LANCASHIRE COUNTRYGOER

Lancashire Countrygoer

JESSICA LOFTHOUSE

Illustrations by the Author

LONDON
ROBERT HALE LIMITED
63 Old Brompton Road S.W.7

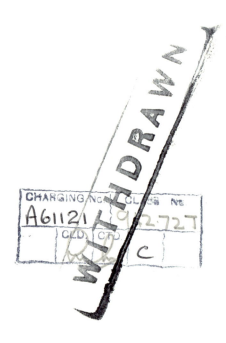
PRINTED IN GREAT BRITAIN BY
NORTHUMBERLAND PRESS LIMITED
GATESHEAD ON TYNE

Contents

Illustrations

Foreword

MY FRIENDS ARE all countrygoers but look at the country in different ways.

Among them are some who rarely walk, look on walking as "an amiable form of lunacy", only dragging their legs—wearied by long hours in the driving seat—out of the car when forcibly made to do so by persistent children or energetic friends. At times they have been persuaded to "look around a village" or visit one of the stately homes of England, or carried a car rug to a picnic spot, but never have they done more than look at a hill from its foot or been the least interested in the promise of a wonderful view. They never mind dropping us for a cross-country walk or picking us up at a pre-arranged spot—which is very pleasant.

Other friends possess cars but have not lost their walking legs. Cars they now use as once they used trains and buses, to "get them there", away from towns and built-up areas to a point where good walking begins. They travel the shortest possible distances at week-ends. Ten or twenty miles they consider enough—then take to their feet.

The rest have never possessed a car but are quite happy in the freedom of the roads provided by the bus services. "Where can't you go by bus?" they ask, knowing the best termini from which to stride away and the best cross-country routes to take them to distant valleys where other buses carry them home.

And what is wrong with the railways? It is good going when Mancunians leaving the city about 9 a.m. can be striding away in the Ribble Valley or ranging the foothills of Pendle about 11. Craven too waits for them and Bowland Forest, after little more than two hours journey.

They all indulge in foreign travel but all realize it is very good to have so much pleasant home ground, such variety close at hand.

Seven of my nine books have dealt with the countryside within easy reach of Lancashire towns, but all have been out of print for many years. "Let us have another," begged my friends. "A book about Lancashire to take when we go off for the day—telling us where to go to escape from the main roads—how best to get there —what we ought to look out for en route—what to see when we arrive." "Road routes and what places to make for so that we can picnic and climb hills and roam round villages and look around old houses," ask the motorists among them who like best to park the car and wander a while. "Walking routes for when we leave the car—or the bus—and have half a day ahead of us," ask the friends who do not use cars and the car owners who do the minimum riding.

We have discussed these "wants". It must be understood the Lancashire countrygoer is not confined within his own county boundaries, but crosses the border because Bowland Forest and the Hodder country, Craven and the upper dale of the Ribble with the mountains of West Yorkshire are all his "by affection". Over the border and the limestone mountains, the high fells, the land of rocks and caves, potholes and waterfalls are his.

Deliberately I have restricted the scope of the book to country within one day's journey, home and back again and time for plenty of wandering and loitering and pleasant "messing around" when the weather is kind enough. Perhaps another volume will follow, of longer journeys—one night away from home—or for those who consider the Lake Country easy distance from their homes and who feel the Yorkshire dales, east as well as west of the Pennines, are their natural "stamping ground".

This is a book of Twelve Rivers, not only Ribble, Calder and Hodder, the rivers of my first book, but the Douglas and Yarrow are in it, the Brock and the Calder, the Wyre and the lovely Hindburn and the Roeburn tributaries of the Lune, and the Darwen and Irwell which, lacking their erstwhile bright waters, make up for what they lack in history and background interest.

Because everyone is tempted to climb a hill when it appears, all the easily attainable heights are here too—Pendle, the Nick of Pendle and Worsa Hill, Longridge Fell and the moortops of Jeffrey, Ganna and Kemple End, Waddington Fell from above Walloper, Cob Castle, Shivering Ginnel and Harrop Fell and many a height overlooking Bowland, Rossendale and Trawden. Neither are the little hills neglected, those the traveller from Liverpool going northwards sees, nor the wild moors the Manchester road user scans crossing the heights of Belmont and Turton, nor the fells which watch the road going from Preston to Lancaster.

For the mountain lover I include the three giants, Whernside, Ingleborough and Penyghent. Their promise, a challenge if you will, was thrown down far away on Turton Moors, their blue heads half way to the sky.

A countrygoer concerns himself with so many subjects beside route finding, map reading and time tables though each of these is "in the preliminaries". There is some bird watching, flower identification; quite an amount of weather forecasting; geology plays its part and architecture too; landscape and scenery are very important, and history which shaped the lives of the countryfolk —and ours. There must be something of all these in a country-going book.

N.B. Urban and industrial matters are completely ignored:

> " Away, away from men and towns
>   To the wild woods and the downs
>   Where the soul need not repress its music——" !

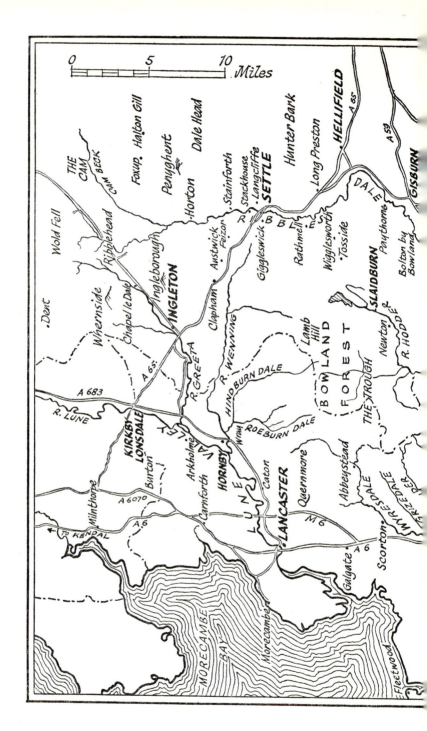

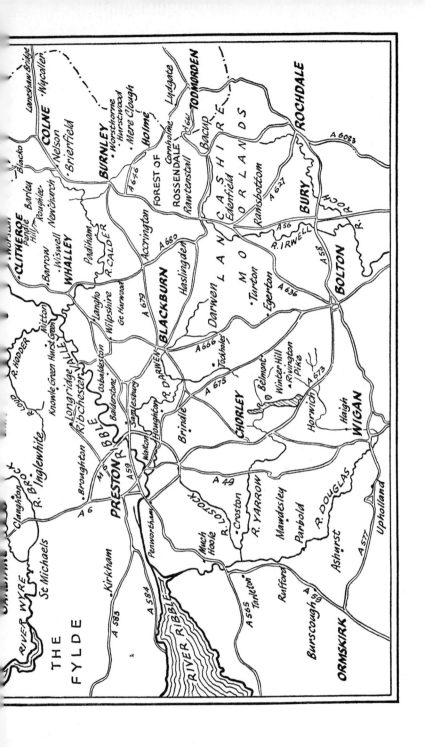

ONE

RIBBLE COUNTRY

Part 1: *The Ribble*

My River and my Native Dale

Byways in the Ribble Valley from Preston to Settle
At Ha'penny Bridge and Samlesbury; Salesbury and
Ribchester Bridge; at Ribchester and Stydd; upriver to
Hacking; at Mitton Bridge; Edisford Bridge; Brungerley,
Hippings and Bridge; from Sawley Bridge to Gisburn; at
Paythorne Bridge; Cow Bridge; updale to Settle

Byways and Fell Roads between Ribble and Hodder
Kemple End to Stonyhurst and Lower Hodder; from Higher
Hodder along Yorkshire lanes to Bolton-by-Bowland

Days and Night Hours on the Fells
Jeffrey and Longridge Fell; at Walloper Well; Shivering
Ginnel

Part 2: *Ribblesdale in Craven*

Craven Ribblesdale
Being bi-lingual; Craven's build-up; Bolton-by-Bowland to
Settle on Craven by-roads; Settle to the source; Stony-
ford and Stainforth; Horton-in-Ribblesdale; to Ribblehead

Three Craven Mountains
Climbing Ingleborough; on and around Penyghent; per-
ambulating Penyghent; the mountain called Whernside;
road routes

Clitheroe Castle, Lowergate and " Wilkin "

I The Ribble

My River and my Native Dale

IT IS IMPOSSIBLE for me to write impersonally about the Ribble, a river which runs like a bright thread through my childhood memories, my first river, the first I came to know from source to sea, following its course with all the pioneering fervour of an explorer. Early intimacy with Ribblesdale has made me a lover of all dale and river landscapes; no scene is for me quite perfect unless a river flows through it.

The border status of the Ribble concerned me not at all as a child. Because it was nearest my Clitheroe home I came to know best the green and tranquil dale between Sawley and Mitton, which since the creation of Lancashire in the twelfth century has been shared by the two counties. Almost continuous riverside paths, from Grindleton bridge to Horrocksford, from West Bradford to Brungerley and Edisford, to Mitton and Hacking Ferry, made wandering easy and we cared little whether we were in our home county or had strayed over the border into Yorkshire—which here lay, contradicting popular opinion, to the west, on the right bank of the Ribble.

Along these " shared " miles there was everything we could desire

—how lucky Clitheroe children are—paddly pools, rock pools for
luring minnows to our nets, little grey-sand beaches, primrose banks,
picnic spots. Here we learnt to look for the grey heron, the white-
bibbed dipper, the kingfisher, and the leaping salmon and silver-
bellied trout. The river never palled.

In this part of Ribblesdale we inhaled history and became conscious of the past without knowing it or giving it a name. History,
folk lore and legend were a happy jumble, with no time sense to sort
out the gay pieces into a pattern or to line up the colourful char-
acters into an orderly cavalcade.

"Gunpowder Plot shall never be forgot, As long as Clitheroe
Castle stands upon a rock," we chanted.

Of course the castle would always be there on its rock; it filled my
bedroom window, we chased around its walls, climbed among the
ruins; for hide and seek there was a Cromwell's Cave for base, and
for adventurous boys to endanger their necks there was a Devil's
Window—like a blind eye in the keep which, said some, was a hole
made by Old Nick when hurling rocks from the Nick of Pendle,
and some said was the work of Cromwell's cannon "from Salt Hill".
We were equally familiar with Old Nick and Cromwell. Cromwell,
"they said", pulled down our castle, crossed the Hodder by the
prettiest of its bridges, and slept one night on a refectory table at
Stonyhurst which schoolboys said "still stank" of him. The Devil,
complete with horns, tail and club foot, once haunted our streets,
waylaid folk, offered three wishes for a soul, and made a general
nuisance of himself until Clitheronians, proving too clever for him,
sent him packing, whereupon he disappeared from sight at Hell Hole
Bridge near Standen Hall.

He shared the scene at Brungerley with poor King Henry. And
in a field near by Nicholas Gosforth, the tailor, kept an eye on a
dun horse which was to help him overcome the Devil. The story
of the Dule Upon Dun was our favourite local legend; it was pleasant
to think a simple tailor could send the devil packing, just as a
Clitheroe parson and schoolmaster had once done by ordering him
to weave ropes out of strands of Ribble sand.

Words of parental caution follow children to the Ribble banks. We
all knew of Peg o' Nell, an evil water spirit, who was particularly
active between Brungerley and Waddow Hall.

Poor Peg! I had a clearer idea of Jenny Greenteeth, the horrid old
witch who lurked far beneath the slimy green weed of all the
Ribblesdale ponds; every Clitheroe child was warned away from
such places, afraid to make closer acquaintance with her.

We knew all about witches; we imagined them on dark nights
careering, broomstick borne, over the big end of Pendle; we pointed

out a witch's cottage in Downham, we ran by a witch's window in Worston, and said we had seen witches in the sky one dark and windy night when we had lost our path near Mearley. We were often witchered—especially when wandering along the exciting, mud-filled, water-logged lanes "under Pendle", we insisted—as everyone did—were Roman Roads. So much did witches play their part in my life I fully believed a witch with skinny fingers somehow was responsible for pulling my feet into boggy places. I was about ten when I discovered a word "wetshod". Previously I had declared, "I've been witchered!"

Romans, Lancastrians and Yorkists, Roundheads and Cavaliers were there on our favourite paths, fighting on our bridges and hiding in our woods and quarries. Witches, boggarts—mischievous imps who lurked in dark lanes, in deserted barns—and fairies, were cropping up all the time. Fairies built the bridge over Bashall Brook, fairies ran in the moonlight up and down the Catsteps in West Clough near Grindleton, and how easy to believe they danced on Fairy Rock on Downham Green!

When my family left the Ribble valley, school holidays saw me back again. Then I gained my first concept of scenery on the grand scale, following the dale into Yorkshire Craven, the exciting and dramatic region seen from afar—from Clitheroe castle walls—as sunlit limestone mountains merging into sunshot clouds, or as a dazzle of snow in winter on the proud heads of the Craven giants, Penyghent, Ingleborough and Whernside.

I remember the great limestone scar where Pudsay made his legendary leap, with the fairy-haunted cave called Arthur's Hole below; I remember Stainforth Force magnificent with the Ribble in brown spate hurling down its rock-steps into the fearsome black cauldron, and the pure enchantment within the gills of Catterick and Scaleber with sunlight on veils of falling water. I learnt to love the lonely uplands too, high in the Pennines, where the Ribble's twin becks, the Cam and the Gayle, are born.

Years later I came to appreciate the gentler beauties of the lower valley, when I was beginning to treat history less light-heartedly and learning to sort romantic fiction from historical accuracy and cold fact.

My love for my native dale is no infatuation—other northern valleys have greater claims to beauty—but from the lonely wilds of Ribblehead, through the Craven hills, in the pastoral country around Clitheroe, and in the rich, comfortable, roomy landscape of the lower reaches, I always find deep satisfaction in every one of its sixty odd miles.

> "If kindly peace be anywhere
> 'Tis surely here—'tis surely here."

Byways in the Ribble Valley from Preston to Settle

"There is no pleasure in travelling except on horseback or on foot. Carriages (and cars) take your body from place to place and if you merely want to be conveyed they are very good, but they enable you to see and know nothing at all of the country."

In this journey through Ribble country the accent will be on byways. A59 is well enough for those in a hurry between Preston and Gisburn, but countrygoers have all the time in the world on their hands. As Richard le Gallienne once said with truth, "Speed is a method by which we miss as much as possible between our starting point and our destination." Shoreditch Public Libraries

Our travels, using our feet whenever possible, begin a little out of Preston, at Ha'penny Bridge. Map travellers need Sheet 95 of the Ordnance Survey.

AT HA'PENNY BRIDGE AND SAMLESBURY

The busy bridge replaced a temporary structure in 1826, this in turn throwing an ancient ferry out of commission. When pedestrian travellers slowly wended their way from Blackburn to Preston in pre-turnpike days the boat at Brockholes had sufficed, but with increased traffic the new bridge with its halfpenny toll was called for. Not far upriver the long motorway bridge of the Preston bypass spans the Ribble not very far from a ford which brought history to this part of the valley centuries ago.

Have you ever thrilled to tales of treasure trove? Then follow the river edge path from the stile at the bridge end and soon you will stand on the SITE OF THE CUERDALE HOARD 15TH MAY 1840, this being the inscription on a low stone.

"Here," wrote a contemporary historian, "workmen carrying excavated earth from the Ribble verge made a discovery of a large mass of silver consisting of ingots of various sizes, many ornaments, silver armlets in good condition, many pieces of silver of various sizes, exclusive of from six to seven thousand coins in great variety, all being enclosed in a leaden chest which, when found, was in a state of decomposition."

What a find! It made headline news in 1840 much as the Sutton Hoo treasure in more recent times.

Workmen then being very much like their modern counterparts "a great quantity of these coins found their way to the public by some means or other", but after a Coroner's Inquest at Preston the find was declared Treasure Trove and allocated, at Queen Victoria's command, to bodies with best reason to be interested. All the coins had been minted before A.D. 928; many were from mints of various Anglo-Saxon kings who ruled in Mercia and East Anglia and others were minted in Gaul and by the coiners of Ludovicus, Carolus Carloman and Berengaria.

Here is a real hidden treasure puzzle not yet solved. Was it a pay chest of retreating Vikings, or loot they were compelled to throw overboard from a galley? A pirate hoard abandoned in a "get-away"? Or was it lost by warriors who had taken part in the Battle of Brunanburgh, when Athelstan's West Saxons fought Northumbrians and Danes, men of Ireland and Strathclyde, and won, thereby welding all England into one? Other counties lay claim to Brunanburgh too.

Ribchester Church

If you would like to see what English country churches were like in the old days, take a peep at Samlesbury's. Few churches are still, like this one, partitioned by calf-box pews of all shapes and sizes, from elbow-to-your-sides two seaters to capacious four-square rooms enclosed by the greater landowners in the parish. In the late seventeenth century each was allowed to appropriate pew space according to his position. Every door is dated and bears a Hall or farm name, or the initials of the first occupiers. Beneath some are family graves—and not unless these are removed can the nave floor, which heaves like the waves of the sea, be levelled as other more ordinary church floors have been.

There is a witch's grave, too, south of the church, with a cracked stone—which "they say" was clamped down by iron bars. Nevertheless "she tried her best to get out!"

At Samlesbury are reminders that Pendle had not the monopoly of Lancashire witches. The local company of witches were fortunate to be acquitted when it was discovered their young accuser—Grace Sowerbutt, a teenage menace, prone to fits, and knowing more of certain things than was good for her—had been well coached in preparing evidence against them, and that it was all a pack of lies.

Had you lived in Lancashire in the early seventeenth century you might have consulted a manual much used by dabblers in the black arts. It contained useful recipes, one for making the human form invisible and airborne. Grace must have heard of it, though illiterate, and remembered certain details when accusing granddam and aunt of seething and boiling the body of a babe stolen from Samlesbury graveyard, presumably at dead of night, and when describing with suitable embellishments how the two women after being carried over the Ribble partook in a wild dance with " four black things going upright yet not like men in the face".

The recipe? To prepare for a broomstick jaunt it was necessary to anoint the naked body with lanoline, prepared from boiled mutton fat, but more efficacious was the fat of a broiled infant. This kept out the cold. Secondly the body was covered with soot from the fire to make one invisible during the midnight excursion. Lastly the magic herb aconite was procured, the drug of which gave the sensation of flying. Modern drugs have the same effect on some.

Beyond the church a winding way called Bezza Lane makes for a farm on the site of the first Samlesbury Hall which, being close to a Ribble ford on the line of a raiding route from Scotland, involved the landowners, especially in the thirteenth and fourteenth centuries, in constant trouble. They erected a stone peel to protect family and dependants when the warning beacons flared from the border south-wards, as they did frequently in the turbulent days of Edward II.

In 1322, Scots on the rampage fired the Hall, looted the church, then away again driving cattle and carrying their booty, leaving death and destruction in their wake.

The Lord of Samlesbury surveyed the damage.

" We'll rebuild," he decided, " away from the Ribble." The site chosen was in deep woodlands which provided seclusion and great oaks for the new timber-built hall. It is still there for you to see though the forest trees have gone, the farmlands near the grounds have been levelled for the landing strips of Samlesbury Aerodrome and the main Preston-Blackburn highway runs against its walls.

Few houses have endured so many vicissitudes and survived. In 1925 it was sold for its timber value, rescued by public-spirited people from the house breakers hands for the sum of £2,750 and now is the joy of many who consider country houses among their country pleasures.

Just under three miles from Ha'penny Bridge the highway, shadowed by trees, haunt of the local ghostly White Lady—for car headlights play strange tricks here—passes the Hall. The pleasant gardens, the splendid Tudor chimneys, the warm tint of the Flemish brick walls and the magpie quatrefoil timbering on the walls facing into what was an inner courtyard are a foretaste of what the place holds in store.

Among the finest rooms in the Hall is the original Great Hall of the late fourteenth century which was provided in early Tudor times with one of the "new-fangled" massive open fireplaces and a most handsome oriel window, the spacious parlour of the same period, for which the mellow-tinted bricks were specially imported, and which has a beautifully ornamented fireplace of more than ordinary interests because of what it conceals. The Hall has a family chapel of 1420 where for generations Southworths, family and household, assembled for prayers, the family occupying the gallery, the rest the ground floor.

Most of us are willing to be diverted by ghost stories. All of us are mightily curious about hides and secret rooms. Here are several versions of the White Lady tale, and the Southworths being staunch papists throughout dangerous days, harbourers of priests, flouters of Elizabethan laws, saw that their home was supplied with concealed rooms.

Ask anyone in the locality and you will hear how Lady Dorothy and her sweetheart, star-crossed lovers, their parents of different faiths, met in secret, arranged a secret midnight rendezvous, how her brothers hearing of the plan to elope parted the pair, fought and left her lover dead beneath the trees. They will tell you that the angry father banished Dorothy to a nunnery, or that she lost her wits, poor thing, or died of a broken heart, or cast herself from her window. Whatever her end, they all agree that the White Lady makes recurring visits to the gardens of Samlesbury. Her night wanderings occasionally upset motorists on the highway and those who sleep within the Hall.

Facts are few and details vague. Lady Dorothy is lost in the branches of the family tree. But two skeletons of young men were found in the moat when the main road was being built in 1826. Who were they? The slain lover and one other killed in the same fight?

The secret rooms are cunningly contrived. They had to be, with itinerant priests coming and going, each in peril of his life, in spite of many disguises and assumed names. One is a cramped place behind the parlour fire, air admitted by a vent, an ingenious pattern of holes in one of the tall brick chimneys easily spotted by one "who knows", and an escape route under the floor and the garden, beyond which the visitor could emerge, the moat behind him and safety, he trusted, ahead.

It was their adherence to the Old Faith in the end brought family fortunes low. The Bradylls who bought the Hall in the eighteenth century stripped some of its fine wood carving, part of the minstrel gallery included, taking it to Conishead Priory where it now adorns the convalescent home of Durham miners.

The highway A59 branches north at the new Five Barred Gate, this being the speediest way to Whalley and Clitheroe. Another route, a very quiet byway with a few bad patches, wanders past Samlesbury Church gate and, reeling like one of Chesterton's rolling, drunken English lanes, finally goes riding high above some of the choicest Ribble Valley landscapes. Jackson's Bank has almost aerial views, lovely as those famed spots above Severn and Wye, where the Ribble's "silver road" coils in mile-wide horse-shoes between pasture and meadow, under wooded banks, round the walls of comely and venerable farms. Nothing is less like the popular conception of a Lancashire landscape than that unfolding above Balderstone Hall, below Alston Hall farm, and about the gentle slopes of Osbaldeston and the dark woods of Oxendale, all of which can be discovered by the wanderer who strays down the tempting lanes forking from the same byway.

Keep to the lane, if you can! Finally you will emerge on A59 by the Feildens Arms at Mellor Brook or the Bay Horse which is but a mile from Oaks Bar, a busy crossroads.

"The tollgate's gone, but still stands lone
In the dip of the hill the house of stone——"

Behind the cottage the turnpike, a stone post, now serves as a garden ornament.

Longsight Road, modern a century and a half ago, goes forward to Petre Arms to join the highway from Blackburn. Down to the valley runs the Ribchester road, and history goes with it.

SALESBURY AND RIBCHESTER BRIDGE

The Ribchester road descends Barker Brow—what an outsize in landscapes, multiform fields seamed by hedges and trees and hardly one acre on the level, the Ribble beautifully coiling, and a blue wall of distant fells—and pauses beyond the New Hall (1667) and the De Tabley where the builders of 1776 flung three graceful arches across the wide river.

Everyone is tempted to pause. What a fair spot it is, and redolent with history. Not only Roman times were eventful just here—though many associate this region with Romans only, as if history stopped the year the legions were recalled—but other periods too had their very stirring days.

Take the Talbots, a local family with a wayside hall at Salesbury, a Ribble bank seat at Dinckley and later, the New Hall near the bridge.

One Talbot helped his kinsfolk at Bashall Hall in the capture of Henry VI in 1464, and received from Yorkist kings his due reward. Another, at Salesbury, plotted at the outset of the Civil War to inveigle local Parliamentary leaders to his Hall for a round-table conference. But, smelling a rat, they came instead to root him out; he fled across the Ribble with his friends, but they gave chase, "pursued them, killed divers of them, took about twenty horses, drove others into the river where the riders were drownded and their horses taken, and having seized upon Sir John's house they found good pillage".

The next year, Salesbury witnessed another pursuit, the Parliamentary soldiers from the Calder and Pendle area following up their surprise defeat of the Cavaliers at Read Bridge near Whalley. They put the Royalists to flight; they made south to the Ribble, their leaders in vain attempting to bring some sort of order among them.

The Roundheads "pursued them to Langho Green—then our Horse came up and pursued them through Salesbury Park and to Ribchester, most of their great ones had some narrow escape and themselves report 'the Horse and Foot took Ribble many wading to the chin'".

For sweet rurality cross the bridge, take the Hurst Green road where Dutton Hall stands in the steep brow of Gallows Lane and come to high level countryside about Dutton. Dutton was named from an Anglian settler, Dudda, his river was Duddel Brook and Dewhurst Woods also take his name. The seventeenth-century hall, pleasant smiling farms, flowers by the wayside and secret woods to get lost in. It is worthwhile going "wonten" on a summer's day hereabouts.

AT RIBCHESTER AND STYDD

A mile from Ribchester Bridge and you come to the village which for two hundred years has been a Mecca for serious and light-hearted lovers of old places. Misinformed enthusiasts of the eighteenth century were willing to believe,

> "'Twas written on a wall in Rome
> Ribchester was the richest town in Christendom."

White Bull Inn, Ribchester

I like it for what it is, an honest to goodness community without any frills or attempt to exploit its undoubtedly rich past. No Ye Olde Praetorium Guest House, or Minerva Café, or Agricola Gift Shoppe about Ribchester, but it has a good, compact Museum of Roman Antiquities, an hour in which is most rewarding.

Tracking down the Romans is fun. Their mark is found in pillars intended for temples but now holding up the porch of the White Bull Inn, the quaint façade of the Stydd Almshouses and the church gallery. You can walk the fort earthworks west of the churchyard, gaze down on granary floor and hypocaust in the Museum gardens, and trace the foundations of a gateway through which the legionaries passed. The pleasant house at the church gates is on the site of the fort commandant's H.Q. Within the churchyard, so green and immaculate, a gem among country graveyards, you may ponder on what lies beneath, on the forms of ritual practised by the Romans within the fort, of many races and creeds and find in the motto carved on the sundial steps food for thought.

I AM A SHADOW, SO ART THOU.
I MARK TIME, DOST THOU?

For three centuries Bremetanacum was an active cavalry fort on Julius Agricola's military highway linking Chester and Manchester with The Wall. The Ribble fort was at the hub of five great roads. The camp was contained within five and three-quarter acres.

As in past centuries when Ribchester was continuously giving up relics of Roman occupation it is still revealing secrets beneath the gardener's spade, but nothing so exciting as the find of a truanting schoolboy in A.D. 1796. This was a fine bronze ceremonial helmet of which the Museum has a replica, the original being in the British Museum where it has pride of place in the Roman Room.

There is a charming bit of eighteenth-century Ribchester around The Hillock, near the White Bull, where markets were once held. Look up for Georgian date stones and well-designed doorheads.

Walk down the river bank for a look—across the water—at the Hall of the Osbaldestons (modernized) which, in the twelfth century, had its "eyries of hawks, hives of bees, cornmills and fisheries of great value". Young sons of the family rode out to win their spurs in the Crusades, in wars in France, Wales or Scotland.

From the lane near New Hotel seek out two interesting buildings at Stydd. The first at the lane side, with its ding-dong bell well and pillared façade, is the "good almshouse" which John Sherburne of Bailey endowed in a will of 1726 "for five poor persons to live separately therein". They do still—five Roman Catholic widows or spinsters, each with home, coals and allowance—and in modern times, assistance of home helps!

Six centuries ago the Knights Hospitallers of St. John of Jerusalem owned an estate at The Stede, a small "monastery" complete with chapel, dormitory, refectory and cloisters. They were crusading monks, rarely at home until the last fighting men had returned from the Holy Places. In 1338—when it was considered it no longer served any useful purpose—it was dissolved.

The barn-like building isolated in the meadow is all that is left of it. But it is our oldest church building in the valley. Look carefully at the north door with zig-zag ornament—the work of the masons in 1136; then round to the south door, its date 1200, considered so beautiful with its concave and keel mouldings, its imposts, abacus and nook shafts, and the flowing grace of its Corinthian leaf forms, that four hundred years ago someone provided the shelter of a porch. They could protect it from the elements—but not from vandals!

The interior is of the simplest—stone-flagged nave and aged oak screen dividing it from the chancel, massive beams and panelled pulpit with cone-shaped sounding board; the only light and heat the sun supplies, through narrow lancet windows.

So far from the village, the church is usually locked and the key stays with the verger in Ribchester. But the parish church of St. Wilfrid has an ever-open door; many think of it as the most impressive in the valley.

The body of St. Wilfrid's is twelfth century. The thirteenth-century chancel, lit by slender lancets, has a squint or hagioscope such as give rise to colourful tales about lepers partaking of Mass whilst being at safe distance from the other worshippers; more likely the aperture was designed for the use of the ringers of the sacring bell; there are tomb lids from graves of Knights Hospitallers of Stydd. The Dutton Chapel, a fourteenth-century addition on the north side of the nave, has trefoil-shaped pillars for its arcading, and a discovery made during wall stripping, a fragment of a mural showing St. Christopher and the Christ Child. In 1405 the Hoghtons founded their chantry and provided it with a lovely, golden patina, oaken screen, at the time the south aisle was added.

There is so much to see and enjoy in the old church. Outside the tall tower surveys all the lower valley. Its bells rang out in times of

Stydd Church

celebration and jubilation, victories and royal occasions. It is at the heart of the countryside now as always.

UPRIVER TO HACKING

From the peace of church and churchyard, up the valley now, over the bridge and into more peace and tranquillity as Nature made it and Man has decided to protect it.

Sale Wheel Woods enshrine some of the most beautiful landscape in the valley, yet in 1959 there was the threat of a large caravan site certain to destroy that which so many come to find. After a Public Enquiry, permission to take the field near by for camping was refused, for here was the quiet and beauty valued by countrylovers, and infinitely precious.

In Spring the seal is put on Beauty when the Ribble in a mighty
sweep or "Wheel" runs between rocks, shadowed by trailing green
tresses of beeches and larches, and the woodlands are a faery dancing
floor carpeted with bluebells.

The path through the wood continues along the river bank, a "fair
mile" for walkers, to a sunny sheltered spot where, in the fifteenth
century, the family of Talbots built Dinckley Hall. The crossing of
the Ribble here was by an ancient ferry. To this secluded spot many
Cavaliers came during the Civil War, sure of safety with loyal
Royalist hosts when they sought the Hall, fugitives, wounded in
battle.

For generations walkers crossed the river by Dinckley Boat but the
ferry, alas! is no more. Storms and floods often swept it from its
moorings to be dashed on the rocks below. The new footbridge, if
less picturesque, is more dependable.

Come on a windy day when standing over midriver you have the
feeling that in a moment you are to be airborne. "Just like Blackpool
North Pier," folk remark, clutching hats and bags. When the river
rushes by in brown spate carrying branches and palings, the rollback
flood waters seem to carry you with them too; very exciting. But
at quiet times peace is here, with gulls on white wings against
blue skies, sandmartins, fluting sandpipers, the cries of curlews and
plover.

Cross the footbridge and Hurst Green and Stonyhurst are only
a mile away. Turn uphill from Dinckley's fields and Tanners Arms
is at the road end, and the byroad linking Ribchester with Old Langho
and Whalley.

In the reign of Mary, men brought stones from Whalley Abbey
then being demolished after dissolution and from the masonry built
a church on Langho Green. Look carefully at the window tracery,
walling stones and carved fragments in the porch. Four centuries
have used it kindly.

Brockhall is near, hospital and estate, but the road onwards soon
comes to a riverside hall in a secluded hollow, like Dinckley, once
provided with a ferry. A farm track leaves the lane, crosses the line
of the Roman road from Ribchester to York, now a grassgrown track,
and away below is the many-gabled house built by Judge Walmesley
in 1607 to replace the ancestral home of his wife, most of which he
chose to pull down. A handsome house it was with its mullioned
windows and tall chimneys, but it soon proved not grand enough for
the Walmesleys, whose main seat was Dunkenhalgh Hall and this
became a farmhouse only.

It "makes a picture" at the foot of the hill with its moat, water-
filled and ice-sheeted on winter days. Even lovelier it is to stand on

the Ribble brink and look back on a summer evening with sun winking in the many windows, cows lowing, the spinning of the fisherman's reel, the chattering of swallows and martins— an epitome of rural peace.

What a page from history is written here!

Romans knew the nearby fords. So did Bronze Age traders one down river. Northumbrian armies fought the Battle of Billangahoh on the banks in A.D. 789 and maybe buried their dead in mounds close by.

Generations of countrylovers have had Hacking fixed firm in their affections so there was much sadness when the Boat was abandoned and no one was there in the Boatman's Cottage to come to their call. More dismay was felt early in 1960 when details of a plan to excavate wide acres near the river bank for sand and gravel were made known, this being part of a precious Green Belt. How relieved countrylovers were when, after a two-day enquiry, the Inspector declared this countryside too valuable a public amenity to allow the scheme to go through!

Some day we hope the Lancashire County Council will find the money to erect the promised bridge, or bridges, and so open up the enchanting Ribble and Hodder side paths again which were our childhood joys and should be pleasures available to generations more.

From Hacking Hall up to the brow once more and the lane goes through the farms of Chew Mill into Elker Lane and A59, not far from Billington and Whalley.

As Whalley is dealt with in the Calderdale part of this book let us pass through the village to meet the Ribble again at Mitton Bridge, where is the most southerly of the five bridges spanning the water between Lancashire and Yorkshire.

AT MITTON BRIDGE

I think the indefatigable Victorian travellers, the Howitts, who wrote of Mitton in the 1840s as "one of the most perfect nooks of the world, one of the places that stand as they stood ages ago, where the slumber of a summer's afternoon lies profoundly as a trance", would not be completely shattered at modern changes. In spite of Macadam's new turnpike road of 1826 and much modern traffic it keeps its rural equanimity. Travellers pass the bridge-end inn, once Mitton Boat when crossing was by ferry, now the Aspinall's Arms, or call in at the Three Fishes—so called because of the abbey stones over the door. Though the Courts Leet are no longer held at the latter as in "good old days" when the village elders chose from among their number constable, pinder, hedger, ditcher, barley-men and ale tasters, there is an old-fashioned air about Mitton, satisfying to those wayfarers who have time to stop, look about them, and consider.

My favourite picture is from the Ribble bank on the Lanca-shire side, through the gate by the Aspinall Arms. Peaceful England truly, age old and changeless. All Hallows, the buttressed gable end of Great Mitton Hall where the priests of Cockersand Abbey lived when they served the church in early days, make a happy composi-tion with green slopes, trees and cattle, and industrious anglers knee-deep in the flowing river.

Three Fishes, Mitton

The twelfth century saw the building of the oldest part of the church and the adjoining building, priests' quarters, belong to the years preceding the dissolution. All Hallows is unusual in having no aisles, and a chancel three steps down from the nave. Its simplicity is very satisfying, for few monuments or murals are on the walls and little distracts the eye from the beauty of the fabric. The roofing timbers are massive beams, the font-cover and pulpit of good Jacobean workmanship. The chancel screen, with its assemblage of medieval carving, cast iron and terra cotta, is something of an ecclesiastical curiosity and subject for controversy.

The chancel has ancient monks' benches, old flooring tiles, a low-side window once used for doling bread and alms to the poor—some like to think lepers were allowed to gather here—and opening from it is the Sherburne Chapel, a fascinating assembly of tombs and monuments well worth an hour of anybody's time.

In 1594 Sir Richard Sherburne of Stonyhurst decided to have built a fitting resting place for his family and descendants. For generations, at Bailey and Stonyhurst, his forbears had worshipped here and many found burial beneath the church. His wife, Dame Maud, was first to be interred in the new chapel and her effigy and Sir Richard's lie in alabaster upon the most splendid table-top tomb with all their armorial bearings on shields on its sides. He was a man of many titles and rode the winds of change successfully through the reigns of many Tudor sovereigns. Among his titles were Master Forester of Bowland, Her Majesty's Deputy Lieutenant in the County of Lancaster, and he was Lieutenant of the Isle of Man also, which probably accounts for his son, who married a Stanley, living at Castletown. Here occurred a family bereavement, the death of the son's wife in childbed at the birth of twins. Her mural monument is very touching; below the kneeling parents are shown twins in their cradle, wept over by nurses.

The Sherburnes of Stuart times, as Roman Catholics and Royalists and Jacobites, suffered accordingly. A later one, Sir Nicholas, who by a marriage to a wealthy heiress was able to recoup the family

Mitton Church and Mitton Hall

losses, employed a skilful sculptor, William Stanton, to make effigies of four seventeenth-century Sherburnes. Stanton's son was called upon when tragedy came to Stonyhurst in 1702 to design a memorial, a mural, telling of the death of the young heir after eating yew berries.

In the vaults below the chapel floor are five leathern coffins studded with brass nails. The smallest contains, in a leaden sheath, the body of the little boy. Beside him lies his mother, on the other side his father, who mourned his tragic death so deeply, and next to them the sister Mary, who became heiress.

Mary first married the Duke of Norfolk and retained the title of "Dutchess" after her widowhood and when she had made a very

secret alliance with a professed Jacobite, the Hon. Peregrine Widdring-
ton. There is a memorial to him, telling that " he was with his brother
in the Preston affair where he lost his fortune with his health by a
long confinement in prison ". But that he had married the Lady of
Stonyhurst—no mention. Only in the vaults is all revealed. The long
coffin of Sir Peregrine is next to hers.

What lengthy memorials she caused to be cut on marble, for her
father " who set the neighbourhood a spinning jersey wool " and
sent for the cottagers to come to a room set apart from them in
Stonyhurst Hall, providing a man to teach them to comb the wool
and a woman to teach them to spin, and for her mother, a true Lady
Bountiful, who provided an apothecary's shop in Stonyhurst where
she dealt out simples and salves, and acted alms giver to her tenants
and the poor about the gates.

More of the Sherburnes and Stonyhurst is in the Longridge Fell
part of this book.

From Mitton churchyard look across to Lancashire and the wooded
grounds of Little Mitton Hall. This house was built in early Tudor
times and for long was home of the Cateralls. If you wish to see the
costume of early Cateralls and their progeny look for the brass in the
north aisle chapel in Whalley Church showing " Sir Raffe who died
in 1515, hys wyfe Elizabeth and all their chylder "—nine sons and
eleven daughters !

Now we turn away from the church on the lanes to Mitton Green,
where is the base of an old cross, and up the valley, hither and
thither with the road, to Edisford Bridge, which is three miles away.

EDISFORD BRIDGE

> "Down the river and over the lea
>   That's the way for Billy and me",

and for generations of Clitheroe children—including myself, when
young.

Long before Clitheroe had a castle, before a bridge was thought of,
the Ford of the Nobleman was in "history". There was a time in
the mid-twelfth century when the unhappy folk of an England torn
by civil strife felt that " Christ and his saints slept "; especially in the
north-west where, with a moving border, no one ever knew just
where Scottish dominion reached, or ended.

In 1137, Scots raiders, under the King's nephew, reached Edisford
by way of the Trough, feeling, as they did in Stephen's disturbed
reign, they had every right to be so far south. The castle Normans
and the local English thought differently, joined forces, and sallied
forth—to be ignominiously defeated at the ford. The raiders were

soon away updale with their loot, into Craven and highroads into Scotland.

In the fourteenth century, increased traffic between Lancaster and Clitheroe made a bridge necessary. The De Lacy estates had passed to the Earls and then to the Dukes of Lancaster; a constant flow of men on Duchy business crossed over, and heavy-laden packhorses and wains bearing goods to markets and fairs in the borough.

Look under the centre arches for the medieval masonry, the ribs of the old bridge. Masons' marks are cut into many stones below and on the parapets; try identifying the work of each man who "wrought" the stones. A bit of detective work!

The Yorkshire end of the bridge was near St. Nicholas Leper Hospital, built after the Crusades for the care and reception of home-returned soldiers suffering from eastern diseases.

Follow the river downstream and you come to Siddows, Henthorn, and after 2¼ miles to Mitton. Turn up to Low Moor and you are in a village created at the beginning of the industrial revolution —"like part of a factory town thrown on to a green hillside" which has stayed as a small village. The mill is silent; no longer are the houses solely for families of mill workers. You may follow the mill-race to The Coe, a weir built to hold up water to be diverted for power; a salmon ladder was contrived—on the Waddow bank, at the same time. The new "river works" caused the water to rise and cover the long-used "Brungerley Hippings". Therefore, in the 1820s, Clitheroe was given a new bridge.

The comment. "And a good thing too! It will put an end to Peg o' Nell and her mischief."

Natural causes would be today's verdict but, before Brungerley had its bridge, every drunken roisterer who slipped from the stones, every daredevil who ventured across when the water ran too high, was claimed as victim of Peg. Her quiet, headless statue stands by a clear spring in Waddow Hall field a few yards from the river brink; she looks harmless enough nowadays. Yet, "She claims one life every seven years," old Clitheronians insist.

BRUNGERLEY, HIPPINGS AND BRIDGE

What an historic spot and not a mile from Clitheroe! Here, in 1464, came a fugitive king, Henry VI, to fall into an ambush laid by the Talbots of Bashall with whose in-laws he had found a brief refuge at Waddington Hall. Maybe he thought to cross the Ribble unperceived and seek the protection of the loyal monks at Whalley. A green river bank, Christian Pighill, now known as Pig Hill, was mentioned as the place of his arrest.

Here too the river spirit of Peg o' Nell claimed her seven-yearly toll of life. And not so far away the Devil flew away on the dun horse!

Brungerley has for generations been a place for children's play, for jam jars and fishing nets, picnics and lovers' loiterings. The path skirts the Ribble edge, the margin a tangle of flowers; tall purple loosestrife spikes rise amid masses of meadowsweet, there is scent of water mint; forget-me-nots and brooklime and red-brown water plantains are at the brink; there are beds of that crowfoot which lies on the river like a snowdrift, and the pale gold and delicately scented flowers of the creeping buttercup. Shoals of minnows glint

Riverside pastures of the Ribble, Brungerley

silver and large fish cruise around in deeper pools, red on their fins. An angler throws a catch on the grass—a wriggling eel!

Such spots we dream of on summer days. I think when Lancashire townsfolk day-dream of country places the Ribble valley comes into the picture; here is some of the greenest of England's green and pleasant land, safe we trust, in the official Green Belt.

But we live in a concrete age and from Ribble edge to Pendle foot is a mile of limestone; so what does the future hold?

Lime, Law and Latin were always Clitheroe's specialities and Lime still looms large on the local landscape. New quarries are expanding but old delphs, like those at Horrocksford, have reverted to Nature.

In silent hollows botanists roam with eager eyes and claim to have found gentians, but I have only spotted the royal blue felwort, tiny saxifrage and rockrose, stork's bill and crane's bill flowering on rocky banks.

Choose either Lancashire bank by Horrocksford and on to Kempstones, or the Yorkshire bank by West Bradford bridge to reach Grindleton. Lanes at higher levels also join the villages and the bridges.

FROM SAWLEY BRIDGE TO GISBURN

Less than two miles from Grindleton a leafy lane drops steeply to the Ribble levels, once the fields of sallow willow which named Sawley.

Sawley's bridge is good to lean upon and dream over the tranquil scene. Sand martins swoop over and under the bridge; still pools are ringed by rising trout and often the arched body of a salmon leaps to the fly. Flag irises are gold in swampy places near the waterside and hawthorn blossom scents the air in May.

In 1147 this sheltered valley was chosen as site for their new abbey by a band of monks, the Abbot Benedict, twelve brethren and ten converts. The hill behind was Mount Saint Andrew. The wealthy lords of nearby lands, some of Norse lineage like Sweyn of Swanside, were willing to grant them tracts near at hand, and others made gifts of sheep pastures and fells in Craven and around the slopes of Ingleborough where for neighbours they had tenants of the abbots of Bolton and Fountains.

For years they laboured, attempted to cultivate the dale, built the great abbey, the church of which towered high above the community of humble cots of the natives. At first conditions were against them. The site was damp so rheums and ague were common. Winters were intensely cold. Distractions made it hard for them to concentrate on praising God. They pleaded to return to Fountains from which they had set out so hopefully. They were prevailed upon to stay.

The abbey was a power in Ribblesdale for nearly four centuries.

The last abbot, Trafford, took part against Henry VIII in the Pilgrimage of Grace and for this treason was hanged. In due course the abbey was dissolved, land and buildings sold, the roofing lead, masonry and dressed stones finding ready buyers. Little was left except rubble core of walls stripped of their facing stones, foundations, and a few of the monks' graves, carved flagstones the curious pause to ponder upon as they wander through the ruins.

The monks diverted a millstream from the river to turn their corn mill. The same water Robert Peel, of the famous Blackburn family which provided generations of cotton manufacturers (and one prime minister), utilised for his early cotton mill, the labour for which he drew from surrounding villages.

Travellers in a hurry go north on A59, now undergoing much widening; reconstruction will soon eliminate that bugbear of a hill, notorious Sawley Brow; this is the highway to Skipton or Settle. Those with time to spare take the pleasanter byroads to Copy Nook, Bolton-by-Bowland and the upper valley. The walker, whose progress is controlled by his whims, has the best of it in the miles ahead, for only on foot can anyone hope to discover the best of this delectable stretch of Ribble.

For me the highspots between Sawley and Gisburn bridges are where Skirden Brook joins the Ribble, the wild woodlands below Bolton Hall where Pudsay's Leap makes a dramatic bit of scenery, the sweep of the river at Denham Wheel.

Skirden Brook and Ribble meet at a paradise for bird watchers. Sit quietly on the bank and let the pied wagtail trot close over the shingle, and the water wagtail flutter its green and gold above a leaf-flecked pool for your pleasure; listen to the sandpipers' calls and the redshanks—in early June. Keep an eye on the acrobatic displays of plovers " giddy with Spring " and the circling curlews giving warning cries to their young, frozen to speckly balls among the brown rushes. Water hens disappear under the bank, mallard dragging their feet across the water rise squawking and fly high over the trees. A heron, " a grey image on stilts ", watches the water, brooding.

The brook crossed, adventuring in the woods brings you to Denham Wheel and the limestone precipice of Rainsber Scar, rarely called by this name since a Tudor Pudsay of Bolton Hall leapt on horseback from the cliff top to escape the long arm of the law. He succeeded too and was granted a pardon from his godmother, Queen Elizabeth, though his crime—minting his own shillings from silver found in his own lead-mines—was a heinous one.

Only slippery paths trodden by fishermen, otters' paths along steep banks, continue through the woods. One discovery is Arthur's Hole, the very cave where the fairies gave Sir William Pudsay the tip about silver coining, wth such unfortunate results. Another, beyond the tree and shrubbery belt, is Fooden, a seventeenth-century farmhouse with a mineral well by its garden wall—where we once thought, after dipping a sixpence in the water, we had found the secret of making coins one stage better than Sir William, gold, not silver.

Out of sight and high level are the remains of Bolton Hall, recently demolished, " the oldest house in Ribblesdale ", was its proud boast; another victim of dread woodworm and dry rot.

The scrambler probably finds himself in a lane near Bolton-by-Bowland and two miles from Gisburn Bridge, a bonny spot, very photogenic and haunt of artists. The lane drops suddenly through tree-shaded banks to open sunshine, a grey bridge, a comely old building known as Gisburn Mill, though it is long since corn was ground here, and the Ribble in its most beautiful setting. In early Spring the steep banks are carpeted with snowdrops; in May bluebells and the starry flowers of the wild garlic cover the ground; in Autumn the river washes through the dipping branches of beeches, flotillas of golden leaves float down the water, and we point out the

Gisburn Churchyard

dark shapes of salmon cruising in the deep pools, lingering on their way upstream to the spawning redds of Paythorne. Their long journey will soon end; they swim under the old walls of the Kennels, once loud with the clamour of staghounds, they leap the weirs and come to the gravelly shallows beyond Paythorne Bridge and at Nappa Flatts.

AT PAYTHORNE BRIDGE

Paythorne's one great day is the Sunday nearest November 20th, when hundreds of interested spectators hope to look in upon the family life of the salmon. Sometimes they are rewarded.

The hen fish is busy scooping shallow grooves in the sandy, gravel of the river bed, laying her eggs and then inviting the waiting cock fish to spread their milt upon them. After which she moves back, with the sole object of covering the now fertilized eggs with more sand and gravel. "And that is that," she says, "until the warm sun of Spring hatches them and the small fry are born and ready to play their part in the salmon life cycle." The survivors will certainly return years hence to the redds where they were spawned.

Paythorne has not the monopoly of spawning salmon; you might see them at Nappa Flatts too—that pleasant stretch of the Ribble where walkers may cross over on the renovated stepping stones and discover the pleasure of rambling over curlew-haunted pastures to farms called England's Head, or Paa and Adams, or striking out on paths ostensibly heading for the retiring hamlet of Halton West.

Keeping to the road, Gisburn to Hellifield, has its merits too. Drop to Halton West Bridge for summer afternoon idling, or turn on the lane at Bend Gate signposted to Wigglesworth, to cross the Ribble at Cow Bridge.

COW BRIDGE

There is nothing much here except for anglers, but interesting country is across the river on the windswept pastures of The Park and Teanlees Hill, which take the walker to Wigglesworth Hall, a "haunt of ancient peace".

Wigglesworth Hall

The Hammerton name is writ large on this landscape. They held much of the Hodder, with their family origins at Hammerton Hall above Slaidburn; they lived here too in a fourteenth-century homestead with a chapel at hand; they erected the stone peel at Hellifield to provide shelter for their dependants when Scots raiders swept through the Aire Gap; they worshipped in Long Preston church and on their tombs there are carved the hammerheads of their family badge.

"From Bowland to the Plains of York we ride our own ground," the Hammertons were wont to boast in their pride. But Sir Stephen in joining the Pilgrimage of Grace ended the fortunes of his family. It was said his son, learning of his father's execution, died of a broken heart.

UPDALE TO SETTLE

In 1753 the local roads from Hellifield to Long Preston and Settle were "amended, repaired, widened", and many buildings en route date from the Turnpike period. The old "Priest Town"—"verra near a mile long to my thinking," as a villager commented—had already earned the title "Long". Its history was long, too, from Roman days when Craven's Old Gate, or Queen's Gate, carried the legionaries over the hills to Scaleber camp, Anglian times when it was a religious centre with resident priest, through Norman days when the church was built—the Tower is massive early work and the font pure Norman—and the monastic period when the Prior of Bolton sent brethren to serve the parish. It suffered from Scots raids, from the "Black Sickness", from storm and flood, to rise again.

History marched on the fell road over Hunter Bark—a walkers' way, a scenic route. By road we travel low level and so, nearing the formidable limestone heights which half-circle Settle, into the old market town.

Come if you can on market day—Tuesday—or on Saturday, when the world and his wife, by Craven dales standard, flock to town.

I have always found Settle, with its odd corners, hoary old buildings and exciting setting, a fascinating place. But changes have come and more drastic clearances imminent. A century ago public outcry saved the Shambles from demolition when the old market square took on a new look; who is to call halt to what is being done now in the name of progress? I trust Cheapside is safe with its Georgian shops, and Constitution Hill and its comely Jacobean and Queen Anne houses, and Kirkgate wandering down its old accustomed eighteenth-century way to the bridge. There is Mr. Preston's Folly, too, now a hardware dealer's, a splendid Jacobean façade planned on too large a scale by an over-ambitious gentleman of Settle, safe as a "scheduled" building.

Whenever I stand on Settle Bridge, now provided with a new foot-bridge so that pedestrians can cross the river without fear of coming to a sudden end, I like to think of the history which has passed over. For over a thousand years history has flowed by on the Scotland and cross-Pennine highway, and for five centuries over this same structure. You can see the medieval ribs beneath, core of the original ten-foot-wide arches.

Byways and Fell Roads between Ribble and Hodder

KEMPLE END TO STONYHURST AND LOWER HODDER

We have travelled from Preston to Settle by valley level routes. Now for high-level travelling, on fell top and fell slope, starting out from Longridge Town and climbing many ridges and heights from which to look down, proudly and highly satisfied, on valley and dale.

Tootill Heights, the White Cross at Newdrop and Kemple End are linked by an hilarious switchback which tipples down Birdie Brow to Higher Hodder bridge after five miles.

Old sites; the silent platform where the Shireburne Almshouses once stood; a battered crosshead on a short stump not far from the Kemple quarries, long known as Paulinus Cross, site of some early long-forgotten missionary journey; Birdie Loan Head where Crom-well surveyed the landscape and found it fair. We do too.

Stonyhurst and its college are so near one can descend quickly from the fell road to the Park and grounds—two miles below.

Here was a great house before the Jesuit fathers took up residence —Stonyhurst Hall.

Early Sherburnes lived in the first part of the sixteenth century at Bailey Hall (now a farmhouse above a wooded clough half a mile or so from Hurst Green Church) but removed to "'Stanyares'", there to rebuild a rather decrepit house already on the site.

Richard (the first of Stonyhurst) left orders to his son Richard the second, to "finish the building therwyth now already begun" and the stately main door was so completed—a great gatehouse in the old style with classical columns.

Because the times were dangerous for Roman Catholics, armorial bearings in stone over the front entrance were made with a cunningly-contrived hole to give air to anyone hidden in the secret room behind.

Cromwell, in 1648, slept (an unwelcome guest) in a hall but half-finished. The third Richard was unable to do much building.

Richard (the fourth) added nothing to Stonyhurst either: he died in Manchester jail for loyalty to James II, but his son Nicholas, marrying a wealthy heiress, was able to carry out the splendid work we see now. He employed some of the finest architects and garden designers available—engineering "canals", designing the imposing new garden gateway, laying out formal gardens with vistas and leaden statues.

The work begun in 1690 was ended in 1717—not with the former zeal shown by Sir Nicholas. His son and heir, in 1702, ate yewberries when playing in the Park and died; his only surviving child was Mary, Duchess of Norfolk. None of the Sherburne name would ever live at Stonyhurst again.

The alterations next to follow were done a century ago by the Jesuits when they knew that the evicted school of St. Omer's was never to return to Flanders or France.

Some well-known names are associated with Stonyhurst. Hansom (of the cab) was called in by the College authorities for plans to enlarge the school. Charles Waterton, the taxidermist, explorer, adventurer, was an early "old Boy". Gerard Manley Hopkins, the mystical poet, was a young priest here and frequently "showed visitors round". Father Rowland, in recent times, was a name known in matters astronomical.

Hurst Green, a pleasant village at the Park gates, well supplied with inns, graced by the transplanted Sherburne Almshouses, stands above a charming Dean. Down below many wheels once turned merrily in a succession of stream side mills. Paths into green glades, by fairy pools, come to Sandy Bridge and a delph from which men long ago used to dig the sand which they sold to Lancashire housewives in farm and town street, in the days when flagstone floors were strewn with sand and innocent of linoleum or carpets. Beyond is Green-gore—King John hunted from here, it is said—and Deer Game Wood.

The highway sweeps down to Lower Hodder Bridges—the older built by a Roger Crossley for the Sherburnes in 1563 for £70, and the newer by John Louden Macadam in 1826. If ever a spot deserves beauty status this does, seen from the bridges looking downwards, or from the Hodder edge looking along the river and through the arches.

Cromwell did *not* cross here in 1648 en route for his battle and victory over the Royalist troops at Preston; there was no bridge then at Mitton so his army must have used Edisford over the Ribble and a higher bridge over the Hodder, one which was replaced by the present Higher Hodder bridge a century ago.

FROM HIGHER HODDER ALONG YORKSHIRE LANES
TO BOLTON-BY-BOWLAND

From the Longridge Fell road we drop to Higher Hodder Bridge, cross and climb to the lane ends, beyond which we strike across a landscape deceptively peaceful. The sunny pastures on the left hand, where Bashall Brook meanders, were a site mentioned in local tradition as the battlefield where King Arthur raised his Pendragon standard and put to flight hordes of warring Saxons, some time in the fifth century. The old grey hall which gazes so blandly upon the same peaceful scene is Bashall Hall which in its day had a life anything but serene.

Six centuries ago the belligerent Talbots settled just here, providing themselves with a band of retainers, ready with horses and arms to fight in national or private wars. Their enmity with the Singletons of Withgill, near neighbours, broke out fiercely during York-Lancaster troubles. Singletons with a hundred armed men attacked Bashall; Talbots retaliated—after eight years.

Their fury for some reason was vented on Alice Singleton, a mortal blow struck by John Talbot " with great malice long thought out ", the weapon being " a lance price sixpence " and to make sure Richard struck her with an arrow " as far as the brain " and a follower " with a stick which would have killed her had she not been slain already ".

Being Lancastrians the Singletons obtained no redress. A Yorkist king was in power—and the Talbots, by helping to capture Henry VI, were in his good books as well as on his pay sheet, for " services rendered ".

Retainers' Quarters, remains of the early hall, seventeenth-century additions and a Georgian garden house at the corner of a green lawn —Bashall has them all, and the last-lived trees of a great avenue which once led towards Waddington.

Some think Waddington the prettiest village in the dale. It is pleasantly landscape-gardened—and cared for by the villagers themselves. The church on its high bank nods at the Hall across the brook. Wayfarers make for its inns knowing they provide good country fare, and many loiter happily and have no desire to hurry away.

The lane out passes the almshouses, the Widows' Hospital (the gateway is 1700), on its way to West Bradford and Grindleton, villages possessing mills yet keeping their own individual rurality.

It is no surprise in this green, wooded, nook-shotten countryside to listen to tales of the fairies of West Clough, who were seen by the Grindleton verger—" little men no higher than my knee with green jackets and caps we' nebs to 'em", who ran down rabbit holes when they caught sight of him !

Like all the best stories told in these parts the date is—unknown.

Grindleton, though in Yorkshire, has a cotton mill, and weaves good cotton too, the Bradford shirtings many of you wear and material manufactured into children's dresses.

The low road from Grindleton continues to Sawley, to Bolton-by-Bowland and routes already travelled updale.

I promised high-level ways, so now for night walking on Jeffrey Hill, an April evening on Ganna Fell, surveying the landscape from Walloper well and Cob Castle above it, and a discovery of Shivering Ginnel and the joys of striding high on Harrop Fell.

Days and Night Hours on the Fells

"Let's go to Jeffrey Hill," say countrylovers on clear and breezy days when the outdoor urge comes in Spring. There is no viewpoint like it, and I think the Roman legionaries pausing for a rest after climbing, with heavy accoutrement, from Ribchester must have looked appreciatively around them. Behind, Ribblesdale and the bare moors unrolling back to Manchester and the far away fort of Chester. Before them the Hodder, the Bowland heights, wilder regions with lurking Brigantes to the north, the string of forts from Overburrow, to Borrow Bridge, Brougham, Penrith and Carlisle.

A mile or so from Jeffrey are lonelier heights which can be reached along paths across the heather, or from the track beyond White Cross which heads to Moorgame Hall or Greenthorn farm. Ahead are the solitudes of Ganna.

Jeffrey is well enough if you like lots of people around. Ganna top is for seekers after space and complete isolation.

I recall an April evening on Ganna—quite alone.

Ribblesdale to the east is green and gold as the sun's slanting rays pour upon it. Pendle, the ever-vigilant, gazes upon the northern scene. Because I know that country so well I can project myself in imagination and memory to the pastures of Pendleton and Mearley and Hookcliffe—where young lambs will surely be running under a sky loud with curlews' cries and lapwings' screaming—where the hawthorn is already in tiny leaf and soon there will be blossom on the wild fruit trees. Downham is hidden at the hill-foot, but I know how evening will be coming to the village—sleepy chirps, cooing doves—tired children being led homewards—the surrounding hills drawing nearer and looming larger in the approaching dusk.

There is a gentle beauty about an April evening over Clitheroe, when the Norman keep becomes a fairy-tale castle rising high above grey roofs—and Whalley Nab, too, is loveliest when spires of smoke rise from scores of cottage chimneys and the sky-line trees grow dim and blue.

To the west under the setting sun is a region where April wears —when she wishes—her fairest face.

The Vale of Chipping at the foot of the fells, gentle, green—a valley of primroses and singing birds and chattering streams and pleasant people dwelling in comely farms and peaceful hamlets.

Above the Loud and the Hodder, all the Bowlands fells brooding as they shut out the dying sun.

A soft blueness falls over the land which a little while before was bathed in gold. The little lambs, their frolicsome, frisky hour of play over, leave their hawthorn hedge race-course, answering the bleating ewes. Soon they will be lying against the warm fleeces of their dams—off-white nestling against darker grey, huddled close against the frosty night air. The rooks have flapped their way homeward.

Returning to the road, I meet motorists, homing too, and possibly, as I am, "filled to the heart with sweet content".

Jeffrey has its quiet times too, midnight and dawn. Have you ever heard of Ned of the Fell, a night rider on Jeffrey long ago? Or met apple-cheeked old ladies who attribute their complexions to "May dewing" up here at break of day?

I have never greeted the dawn of a May morning on these fells but once with a friend I did wait for the June sunrise on Jeffrey.

JEFFREY AND LONGRIDGE FELL

"Night is a dead, monotonous thing under a roof," wrote R.L.S., "but in the open world it passes lightly with its stars and dews and perfumes."

How right he was! Our night on the fells was memorable. After breaking down family opposition and professing to turn a deaf ear to comments about the madness of our intentions we determined to enjoy our night "under the stars". The weather was co-operative, a warm, balmy night after a spell of hot, sunny days.

A late bus dropped us in Longridge Town at 10.30. Men and women were still gossiping at cottage doors and lingering at their garden gates, unwilling to end a perfect day too soon. The air was balmy. The sun was slowly "making a golden set" which has always been "token of a goodly day tomorrow".

As we started out along the fell road beyond Tootil Heights the nearer features of the landscape resolved into silhouettes. The black shapes of cows, sheep with their lambs and a large hare, its long ears pricked for sound, all were clear-cut against a rose gold sky.

Especially lovely were the waving grasses—they reminded me of a Dürer print—on the bank tops above the black walls, and the moon-like pallor of dog daisies in meadows, and guelder flowers and elder blossom at the road edge. We saw owls on the wing in silent flight from barn to tree; curlews also winged by, calling, with the sunset behind them, and we heard a drumming snipe and saw it sweep downward to the dark earth.

Westwards, the coastline resolved itself into a girdle of bright lights where, on miles of brilliantly lit promenades, thousands of holiday makers were doubtless strolling. White lights and yellow, orange and red, outlined the sea verge from Fleetwood to Lytham St. Annes, while towns like Preston disclosed themselves by thick clusters of brighter twinkling lights, in green and gold.

Soon after 11 p.m., the moon had risen, a huge, three-quarter moon with a foolish face like Humpty Dumpty, red at first, then pale as an egg when it had climbed high into the sky. It was bright as a battery of flood lights and by it we found the best place—by that sheltering wall which runs along the fell top—to rest. The thickly cushioned turf proved the softest bed.

> "Under the great evening sky,
>   Across the wide semi-circle of dark land,
>   Small and desolate, here and there are homesteads
>   Tiny, alone——"

Pricked out by single lights we could tell where lay Thornley and Wheatley farms, Hesketh End and Houghclough, Elmridge and Countess Hey. Chipping disclosed itself by twinkling cottage lights. Then, one by one, the lights went out and only one winking car headlight wove in and out of the trees at Leagram.

When a cold night wind blew up we sought a sheltering wall above Meg Hall. Only by the soughing sound, like waves of the sea, did we know that wind tossed the boughs of the trees at the farm.

At first, silver veils of mist blew into the moon's face with great rapidity. Then the moon paled, the stars became brighter and the sky was a deep, dark blue. By midnight the hills had gone, the valley was a pale blur of mist.

We must have slept. Then came that "stirring hour" when as R.L.S. wrote, "a wakeful influence goes abroad over the sleeping hemisphere, an inaudible summons, a gentle touch of Nature" and we felt rather than saw that day was about to break.

No two dawns are the same. I was waiting for the call of the first single watchful curlew, the true herald of the day. But no clarion call came. The moonlight waned, the stars dimmed, a silvery light spread above the fell—and still no curlew, no lark, no cuckoo, no small birds' reveille.

With a dramatic burst, out of silence, came a full chorus, every bird going it. No doubt about it; day was launched.

At 3.30 we dropped to the valley at Thornley, through swathes of mist which lifted to unclothe a world of trembling dew drops, honeysuckle-draped hedges and wild roses. And no soul stirred; no farm dog barked.

At 4.30 the sun came up in a dazzling blaze and the Vale of Chipping was charged with glory. We blinked and shaded our eyes.

A little later came the sound of a mowing machine being started up; the first farmer was beginning his day's work. Haytiming was on at Hesketh End.

AT WALLOPER WELL

Names on the map of our fells intrigue me. What of Cob Castle, Darking Pot, the Duckpit, Old Ned and the Wife, all near familiar Walloper Well?

Walloper Well; a spring of icy cold, crystal clear water, which is what " walla " means. Popular opinion for a century or so preferred a more picturesque derivation.

> " The mason who built it, in love with a maid
> Who brought him his dinner, one day, so 'tis said,
> Was struggling to kiss her, when over the fell
> A pedlar then passing, cried ' Wallop her well ! ' "

There is also the story of a henpecked husband encouraged to silence a nagging wife by a passing pedlar. " Wallop her, wallop her, wallop her well," he said.

Climb through the heather and above the shooting butts and you soon come to Cob Castle on the tops above the well. The name suggests that this was site for an earthwork or defended camp, possibly in Celtic times. What a comprehensive view you get from this point, the best I know, with the sea, the Pennines, the Bowland Forest watershed and the Craven mountains as the limits, all in one tremendous sweep !

On the fell ridge is Whitestonecliff, so often mentioned in forest perambulations of Bowland—" From Harrop Dyke by Fellbrigg Water to Start Haw and as heaven the water deals to the north end of Whitestonecliff, so to Woodward Score, the head of New Hey, by the Duke's lands and Bashall Land to Bashall Park "— such was a border survey when Bowland belonged to the Duchy in the fourteenth century.

Linger here on a clear blue day when breezes bring up the squawking of wild duck from the Duckpit—Browsholme Tarn was a decoy pond—and the sweet notes of rock-hopping titlarks and fluttering pipits. If the day is cold there is shelter against the highest wall and you watch dappled white clouds float by, giving a filmy cap to Pendle, or draping the pointed fells of Airedale or the mountain tops of Craven.

The height of felicity? I think so. Few walk here nowadays though an old track makes for Hare Clough and Browsholme (very wet). I have heard tales of a fell-track tavern kept by Red Ned and a

View towards the Hodder Valley from Walloper Well

stream of shepherds, wild fowlers and lead miners who called as they went by.

Across the road from the well starts a path over Easington Fell to Slaidburn. It crosses a gap in a bank which long ago acted as dam for a pond; the water was used in the lead ore separating process known as "hushing". Another reminder of lead-mining days is the name Smelt Mill Clough given to the exciting ravine with its rock walls and rowan trees which descends towards Underhand farm, with the fell road for company.

When a geologist gazes on the Hodder scene his eyes light on primeval seas, on coral reefs rising from ocean beds, whereas we see only a land of green pastures such as the psalmist sang of, with knolls like Dunnow Rock, Sugar Loaf, Bluebutts, Boarsden, crowned

with beeches, and the pattern of farming like a patchwork cloak
thrown about their feet. It is a landscape deeply satisfying.

The green glades once sheltered the deer at fawning time; the fields
of Heaning were fenced off in the grass-growing months at the
verderer's command, the smooth, sweet upland pastures were
imparked for the fattening of the deer for venison; pockets of land
divided from the rest were vaccaries for grazing of the kings' dairy
cows—and the abbots' cows and calves fed on the slopes in the upper
dale—we know all this. When we hear a farmer calling up the cows
at milking time this is a sound which has never changed since men
have lived in Bowland.

Nothing changes, we believe. A young farmer comes striding
effortlessly down the fell to the Walloper road, using his long crook-
handled stick, a sheep dog following close behind. A shepherd at one
with the hills—he pauses, scans far horizons, and becomes part of a
scene which is timeless. Then, dog at heel, he makes for a smart car,
hops in and drives down the road !

Once the smoking chimney used to be sign of life at fell farms.
No smoke—no one astir. But not now.

" Fires in t'morning early ! Nay, when we want to brew up it's
electric kettles now," was the greeting when we arrived at a farm
door at 7 a.m. after a night out of doors.

But this belongs to the Hodder country; more of this in its own
section.

SHIVERING GINNEL

Large-scale maps show Shivering Ginnel on the felltop above
Harrop and Grindleton. If names intrigue you, then off you will
hare to the hills, wondering.

A Harrop Fold farmer told me it was a short cut to the Old
Bolland Gate and West Bradford. Old Bolland Gate is worth finding,
too, a lane like a tunnel beneath arching trees and between high
hedges which makes direct to the fells and Heys Farm, with its
memories of the time when it entertained Gandhi and brought to
attention all the rural constabulary.

On the June day we sought the Ginnel it was anything but
shivering, the way was all blossom and perfume from Smalden Lane
to Asker Hill, where butterflies fluttered ahead of us.

Hollow ways and deep-rutted tracks took us from lower to higher
farms, then over pastures where frantic curlew parents warned their
speckled offspring to lie " doggo". A high stone wall was ahead,
concealing The Ginnel. Climbing a gate, on the 1,000-foot contour,
we jumped into it, just a grass-floored track pent between the

wriggling, broken-down walls which some eighteenth-century land-owners enclosed from the wilds.

How wide is this Shivering Ginnel? A large flock of sheep could be gathered into it; drovers could let large numbers of beasts graze within it. Many quarries are to be found on the fells around; transport from these stonepits must have used it a century ago and more.

Like the oldest, forgotten ways this was waterlogged, with rush-beds and pools hindering our progress. But what a view; for the Ribblesdale landscape it is worth climbing so high, and to look on Clitheroe mapped out, grey and green, and Pendle brooding behind.

We were soon to witness a rare spectacle—an invasion of birds in a dark cloud, silent on the wing. They circled, came lower and suddenly hundreds "let" on the walls of Shivering Ginnel whilst hundreds more flew down to a still pool. They were all prompted by the same urge, rose together, then fell together, all facing to the south-east. Two angry plover resented their intrusion and rushed in to the attack, whereupon the birds rose, circled, then in a black cloud made for Pendle. Fieldfares, the last of our summer visitors.

Craven farm, Crummackdale Head

II Ribblesdale in Craven

Craven Ribblesdale

ARE RIBBLE VALLEY and Ribblesdale synonymous?

The Valley takes the mature Ribble down to the sea, the Dale cradles the infant river in the mountains of West Yorkshire and its fells watch the stripling river leap down towards Settle and the county boundary.

The distinction is useful historically as well as geographically. In its time the Ribble has acted as boundary between the Celtic kingdoms of Cumbria and Scottish Strathclyde, between Northumbria and Mercia in the days of the three kingdoms, between Eurwicshire and Chestershire before Lancashire existed. It was always a clear language barrier.

BEING BI-LINGUAL

We do not always realize we speak two languages as far as place names go, we who live in the north-west, speaking Anglian and Scandinavian fluently.

To prove it, just study the names on Sheet 90 of the one-inch Ordnance Survey. You are familiar with all, Anglian and the Scandinavian, Norse and Danish.

Take path-finding. In Lancashire, south of Swanside Beck and east of the Ribble, we wander by Brooks, scramble up rocky Cloughs, by noisy Waterfalls. We stride across the Moors, loiter by lonely Pools. Driven to shelter we seek Barns or crouch against the walls of a convenient Sheep Fold. But in Yorkshire, in Ribblesdale north of Swanside Beck, we leave Anglian names for another language. Now we roam by Becks, scramble through deep Ghylls or Gills loud with the roar of Fosses or Forces. Crossing the Fells we startle wild fowl from lonely Tarns. When rain sweeps over we rush for a Laithe or seek the leeward side of a Bield.

The Ribble and Ings Beck must have been a line south of which the Scandinavian-speaking settlers did not advance. Their "Wicks" which were dairy farms, their "Bys" which were villages, you find in the Dale. The "Berghs" and "Barks" named the rocky hilltops near their homes, and the "Bers" their enclosures; many in Craven.

A Seata, as in Norway, was a summer pasture—so are the Setts and Sides. Skali or Scales were huts. An Erg or Ark was a hill shieling where herdsmen cared for the dairy cattle.

Their cleared land was a Thwaite, their lowlying river-level fields were Holms. Hause or Hawes was a defile or pass between hills; a Slack was a dip or shallow valley.

Look on the map of the West Riding, the Ribblesdale area. For a few examples of each there is no need to scrutinize long. Giggleswick and Austwick, Hunter Bark and Stainforth-under-Bargh, Oxenber, Yarlsber and Bookilber. Settle and Swanside, Winterscales and Cow Ark, whereas any farmer talking over field names deals in few which are not Scandinavian. Good fun for a winter evening, listing the names under their two language headings.

CRAVEN'S BUILD-UP

Craven is to geologists very Heaven. To spelaeologists it is a happy hunting ground. To mere countrylovers it is a region of rare beauty, attaining splendid proportions with its contortions, grimacing, and primeval "mountains of the moon" landscapes.

Every book dealing with geology and scenery has chapters on the mountain limestone of Craven which we are told was formed on the bed of silent, shallow seas long before our islands were in existence; bones of sea creatures were deposited to a depth of three thousand feet in parts of the ocean floor. At Clitheroe it was almost one mile thick.

It is limestone's nature to split in clean joints at right-angles to its bedding plane; it is soluble in rainwater: therefore its narrow cracks by water action widen into those ankle-wide clints and leg-wide grikes which makes walking across the bare-as-bone plateaux of

Moughton and Norber above Horton-in-Ribblesdale, above the rim of Malham Cove, on Storrs Common below Ingleborough—and on a score of other fells, so hazardous. Pity the poor wanderer benighted in such places.

Rare flowers, out of the reach of the most ardent uprooter, bloom in deep clefts. The commonplaces are masses of geranium robert, yellow toadflax, red valerian and harts-tongue ferns in lesser clints, fine ferns and foxgloves make gay the larger, whilst the widest gaping rifts give roothold for thorns, rowans and maybe a yew or holly. Approach the lip on a spring day and a great fluttering of wings follows; small birds find nesting holes within. In Winter all one hears—a croak from a carrion crow!

Craven streams have the tantalizing habit of taking, without warning, to the ways of darkness. The Dee does a disappearing trick in upper Dentdale; the little Skirfare vanishes under its own bed half-way down Littondale, allowing us to walk the water-smoothed pavements as down a well-paved road. In Spring trout are happy in deep pools; then comes a dry spell and the poor fish are left gasping in isolated potholes, stone basins in the river bed, there to die unless rescued and taken to lower reaches where the river runs as rivers ought.

The River Aire misses a grand opportunity to make a great splash. Just south of Malham Tarn, at Water Sinks, the streamlet destined to be the Aire percolates into the rocky ground when it ought to run down the Dry Valley to plunge in a spectacular cascade, 300 feet drop over The Cove.

The Ribble, unlike sister streams which follow Persephone into the dark kingdom of Pluto, prefers to remain in the sunlight of the upper world; now—but long ago Cam Beck dropped into a pothole, passed into subterranean blackness and was there confined, until after some great disturbance the cave roof fell in. And that gave us Ling Gill.

Range the slopes of Penyghent and many a small beck you will see plunge into a gaping pothole. Many potholes on Ingleborough's side swallow up mountain streams. Whernside is riddled with water-sinks and swallow holes.

Nature at every turn worked on Craven with theatrical effect, grand-opera scale. She did not create a nice bit of scenery here, a pretty bit there; she hurled great slabs of scenery about—and the Craven Fault, why, that is a forty-mile belt of linked wonders—surely a land "fit for Nordic heroes to live in".

How the Craven Fault (with two more minor disturbances) upset the geological apple cart, forcing up the old beds of limestone so that they are a forty-mile wall, cliffs, ramparts, scars, rising dramatically—all limestone's moods are full of drama—above the younger and very humdrum gritstones which in the natural order of things lie upon the limestone.

From Kilnsey Crag, looking upon Wharfedale, to the fells above the Lune valley there is not a dull or off moment, scenically. Gordale Scar—another collapsed pothole and roof-fallen cave—the semicirque profound of Malham Cove, the gorges and waterfalls of Scaleber, Catterick, Stainforth, and the roaring forces in the glens of Ingleton, the rock-walled silences of Attermire, Warrendale, Giggleswick Scar and the precipices of Moughton and Norber—all these are obvious and need little searching for, but they are only a beginning.

The Celts gave Craven its name—Craig-vaen, the land of rocks. The Scandinavian Wapentake of Staincliffe had the same meaning.

Above the fells and dales, three giants lord it over all the tops of Craven; Whernside, Ingleborough and Penyghent. 2,419 feet, 2,373 feet and 2,273 feet—they have no competition, Pendle not even reaching the mountain status—169 feet short!

Actually there were three Craven faults to make the landscape more complicated, and interesting, but when we come to the three Craven giants their geology is much more well-organized.

Ingleborough, standing firmly on a base of rocks over three million years old, and some even older, obeys all the rules. The second stage, built up on top of the Ordovician and Silurian slates, is of carboniferous limestones—the flat limestone pavings, cut by countless crevices called clints and fearsome rifts called potholes, we walk across most carefully near Crina Bottoms and Storrs Common; this ocean-bed limestone is the thickest layer in Ingleborough's architecture. Next comes thinner strata, in threesomes—shale, sandstone, limestone—repeated in that order with appearance of thin seams of coal. For centuries local folk worked outcrops of coal on their own land.

It is a shock to find coal pits near the Pennine watershed, to come upon a Coal Gill in Whernside, small pits on Penyghent—and a colliery village at Ingleton, built in 1913 though the New Colliery closed down after twenty-five years.

Coarse gritstones make up the top layers. Millstone Grit gave its name to Whernside—the site where querns were quarried, it gives Ingleborough its lion's head and Penyghent its frowning brow.

Each rock is responsible for its own scenic effects, and its own distinctive flora and bird life.

The mountain limestone gives me most pleasure. My seventh heaven is a fell slope, close-bitten by nibbling sheep to the smoothness of a lawn, where the scent of crushed thyme follows us, and so many flowers adorn the pastures—the delicate mountain pansies, yellow and purple, the bird's e'en or mealy primrose, fluttering

yellow rockrose and heartsease, cowslips and purple orchises. These
are the commonplace flowers of Spring in Craven.

I love the lost lanes too, almost choked with flowers; they shelter
the earliest primroses and violets, aromatic and snowy masses of
Sweet Cicily, Canterbury Bells in pale lilac spikes, clumps of the
blue meadow cranes-bill, crimson bloody cranesbill, and the tiny
dove-foot trails over the old stones. Bright runnels have to be forded,
margined with brooklime and forget-me-nots and the spotted monkey
musk; marigolds grow there and sometimes the paler, golden globe
flower. They are cressy rills. Bistort, the pink passion dock; Easter
magiant, much used by dales women for making of herb puddings,
blooms in damp hollows.

Botanists discover a hundred more, rarer flowers. But these content
me.

BOLTON-BY-BOWLAND TO SETTLE ON
CRAVEN BY-ROADS

I suppose when we visualize the perfect English village we picture
one with a village green, well-disposed cottages around its edge, maybe the church tower surveying the scene with the serenity of ages,
with the inn as a convivial and focal point—and with cross and
stocks to remind us of the not-so-pleasant customs of what we choose
to call the good old days.

Bolton-by-Bowland has all—most delightfully placed so that to
wander round the village is a most pleasant way of spending a
summer afternoon. It has two village greens—the upper one beyond
the church is enlivened during playtime at the nearby village school
by youngsters who overflow from the restricted space of the official
playground and continue their games on the grass and in and out the
chestnut trees.

The Bowland courthouse and residence of the local arm of the law
is almost too pretty a place, with its seventeenth-century doorhead
and creeper-covered walls, to associate with the punishment of
wickedness and vice—as it did until recent years.

The lower green has everything the perfect village should have :
a cross with steps and stocks, all broken, it is true; a green, though
the grass is usually like a hayfield; a lovely little memorial garden
with a brook flowing behind its bushes; and the church with its
long nave roof and pinnacled tower looking down from a high
platform of land.

All around are comely seventeenth- and eighteenth-century cottages with charming gardens. To complete the picture is the inn with
a sign of the Coach and Horses.

In the old church look for Sir William Pudsay's font, for Sir Ralph Pudsay's tomb in a chancel arch—the knight, his three (consecutive) wives and his twenty-odd sons and daughters all shown on a slab of black Craven limestone polished like marble. Look for other memorials in the Bolton Hall chapel and examine the very fine carvings on the pew doors, mostly dated 1694. Near the church are paths stepping down to the stream and wandering in and out of cottages.

If you travel the 11 miles of byroad linking Bolton-by-Bowland and Giggleswick on Tuesdays or Saturdays, you find knots of women at every lane end, waiting for the twice-weekly bus to Settle market.

On days other than market days the lane is almost deserted. You pass into a windy world with a few pockets of sheltered calm.

Village street, Bolton-by-Bowland

Forest Becks lies low by its becks and bridges; Wigglesworth school looks ready to be carried off in the teeth of the wind and the village is swept by clean and invigorating breezes. Curlews are blown across the pastures above the Hall of the Hammertons and above lonely farms scattered over the open countryside.

Rathmell stands high; it had to, for the valley was a vast swamp, like a lake when the Ribble overflowed its banks after a cloudburst.

At first glance here is an " un-especial " place—stone-built cottages and farmhouses in amicable proximity, all under the same wind-breaking girdle of tall sycamores and great ash trees, sharing the same sunny hilltop, their doors and windows opening on to wide and lovely landscapes, to the long blue fells, to the low and flat " Ings " of the valley floor, or to the dazzling limestone scars and sky-reaching mountains at the dale head. But Rathmell with its Celtic name is old; there are Celtic sites on the hillside northwards called Brackenny Brow; Norseman farmed here and a certain Carl, owner of ploughlands, is in the Domesday Book. A row of four cottages at College Fold, with a garden overspilling flowers in front and a date-stone R.F.E. 1686 behind, was Dr. Richard Frankland's Nonconformist Academy in 1670, one of the first of its kind and cradle of congregational training for the ministry.

At Rathmell also lived the farmer who woke up one morning far from home lying on a haystack which had been his bed after a bout of hard drinking—and found himself surrounded by " furriers ". Where did he come from? He gazed around him, sorely puzzled. He did not realize his soft bed had moved bodily in the night, lifted by the rising waters of the Ribble after a storm, and had floated downriver before settling on the banks. He was in unknown country. To make his own place of origin clear he shouted, " I come fra Rathmell—Ra'mell in England." The name has never been forgotten, nor the story, though " ings " denote low-lying fields.

The road drops suddenly to proceed, within walls, to Giggleswick. But if you want to get off the beaten track, reaching Giggleswick roundabout, fork left in Rathmell. Choose a summer day during haytime—quite the best time. Pause awhile by the dreaming pond, by the old saw mill, which has been flour and cotton mill in its time, then allow yourself to be beguiled into a labyrinth of lanes.

The way begins well, then, narrowing between high hedges tasselled with hay tugged from passing carts, the lane goes " wonten ". Honeysuckle and purple vetch drape the bushes, harebells, betony, knapweed and scabious cover the banks; you climb between brambles and raspberry bushes, find whinberries for the picking against the old walls. Then you twist and turn wondering what the next bend hides. There is Sheepwash farm, Wham high in its windbreak, Rouster and Farther Rome. Another farm called Rome is nearer Giggleswick as the lane escapes from the wild fell country to pass sedately through lush fields and the contented mown and gathered meadows.

Giggleswick; what a good thing the main highway left it alone when improvements cut through Settle—an eighteenth-century by-passed village. What a funny name! strangers say. The river too—the Tems? Ever heard of a Mr. Clutterbuck of Biggleswade who sent luggage in advance to Wigglesworth via Giggleswick?

Ghikel was probably a Norseman whose " wick " or farm was here. Also the ebbing and flowing well, not so far away, was a " gugglian " or bubbling spring; the wick by the gurgling well could be a derivation. But who cares—or whether or no there was a Saxon Princess martyred at the hand of pagan Danes to give St. Alkelda's its name. Or was the well where the Celts worshipped a spirit of water, later sanctified as a holy well, and as the " halig keld " did it give the first church its unusual name?

This is the kind of village one dreams about. The church lies low with a cross near its lych gate, seventeenth- and eighteenth-century dwellings close about it and a peace disturbed by nothing more than cawing rooks, the Tems babbling and the clock marking the passage

Giggleswick

of time. It is eminently a place to wander round, along back lanes, on paths in and out of groups of cottages, admiring the pleasant pictures the church makes from many unexpected angles. Inside the church—a typical Craven type with a long roofline, west end tower to east window without the break of any screen or chancel arch. The Jacobean wood carving on the panelling of the pulpit and church-wardens' pew—" The standardes of the children of Israel when they to Canaan cam "—and the Pore Box, are particularly good.

From the quiet village street and up Bell Hill, suddenly we are faced by the humming traffic of the busy highroad from Settle to Ingleton and Lancaster or Kendal. Escape is possible on less noisy ways northwards, from either end of Settle Bridge.

SETTLE TO THE SOURCE

We are only ten miles from Ribblehead with two roads to choose between as far as Helwith Bridge—both quiet after the broad high-way—beyond which it is everyone together, road users, mountaineers and potholers all heading north by the same route.

The same route but different goals. Wanderers make for three peaks, taking them together or singly—to Horton for Penyghent, to Selside for Ingleborough, to Ribblehead and Blea Moor for Whernside.

Freedom to change one's mind is among the joys of taking to the open road, R.L.S. said with truth, and here is every temptation to change one's direction a score of times.

Attractive hamlets and villages delay us. Stackhouse with beech woods behind it and creepers staining the walls of old houses in Autumn is the first, on the west side of the dale. Centuries ago it was home of the Carrs and fortunate families live now in the same lovely homes fronted and flanked by gardens which seem to have come straight out of the covers of glossy gardening magazines. Just behind, through the wood and on to the limestone pastures, a path climbs along the skyline, linking the burial mounds of prehistoric hill men. At each gate curious stirks wait for us, or race to meet us with tails raised and ready for a boisterous welcome. From the highest knolls —behold, the mountains of Lakeland, far away!

A mile or so north of Stackhouse the seventeenth-century hall of the Watsons watches two roads, ours and the ancient one coming up from the old one-arched bridge over the Ribble. A stony track which soon degenerates into a grassy path climbs due west, over the pastures to the enchanting hamlet of Feizor. Knight Stainforth Hall has always been at the meeting of the ways near an important river crossing.

The curious, rambling to Feizor, notice the rocks of Smearsett Scar half way and, climbing for the view, find the sheep feeding on close-bit turf sprinkled with thyme and eyebright, potentilla and bird's foot trefoil. Celtic herdsmen probably watched their flocks on the same height, but who raised that great wall of huge limestone slabs, and why, no one knows.

Langcliffe is on the east side of the dale, not far out of Settle. The village proper, around its green with fountain and Big Tree, is missed by those travelling the road updale. But Langcliffe Hall at the road side, an elegant walled-in mansion of the same Dawsons who entertained Isaac Newton—did he ponder on apples and gravitation in the garden summer house called Newton's Arbor?—no one passes without a curious glance.

The village has an air of completeness. It looks very good spread out below as we climb the fearsome hairpin bends on the road signposted to Malham via the Tarn. This site, according to a local tradition, was chosen for the new Langcliffe when an older village was deserted. Was the site of the "forgotten" Langcliffe on the broken ground nearer the river, and were the raiding Scots to blame for its destruction? Or plague?

North again and we come upon Stainforth, distinguished as Stainforth-under-Bargh.

STONY FORD AND STAINFORTH

At Stainforth the Ribble, more like a brawling mountain torrent between rocky, tree-clad banks, over a boulder-strewn bed and arched most beautifully by a one-span bridge, is pure enchantment.

Stainforth Bridge, an ancient Ribble crossing

The magic holds—in Spring when the woods are part of Faery; in summer when the shoutings and laughter of bathers above the Foss, and swimmers below the Foss, make the welkin and the valley ring.

Standing on the sun-warmed parapet of the bridge we watch and are dizzied by the under-and-over, in-and-out-the-window sport of swallows and sand martins. Winter holds black magic when thunder of the Foss in time of spate has a "mile long voice", and we recoil at the sight of the curdled, frothing waters and the sinister aspect of the witches' brew boiling in the black cauldron.

In June we watch the movements of dippers feeding nestlings in crannies within the same cauldron wall, and look on as queues of young salmon below the staircase of rock ledges make their repeated attempts to leap into the calmer waters above the top step. "If at first you don't succeed—", admonish those elders who have leapt the Foss before.

In monastic times when Fountains and Sawley abbeys had large estates in west Craven this bridge was built; the good, firm river bed, the stony ford—in Norse the Stain Forth—had sufficed from ancient times. This is more important-looking than the usual pack-way bridge, but it served the same purpose.

Many routes converge today at the ford, but they are never so busy as in the days when they carried the trade and transport of the two rich abbeys. They are good walking, all of them, from Kilnsey Crag and over Mastiles Lane to Malham Moor, Sannet Hall and Catterick, or from Clapham and Austwick via Feizor and Knight Stainforth.

Who passed by? Agents concerned with abbey affairs, stewards thinking of accounts to be rendered for sheep walks and granges, tenants carrying rents and dues, in kind, to the abbey cellarer, and outlying parishes sending grants of tithes to the abbots' storehouses. Drivers came with long trains of packhorses carrying loads of wool, fleeces, hides and skins, lead and lime, peat and salt, from the west towards Fountains, south to Sawley.

And the clamour when flocks were herded along to be counted, sorted, washed and clipped at the Friar Stainforth Grange, and when, in both Spring and Autumn, great movements of sheep were expected, the coming and going of Fountains flocks from their summering pastures in faraway Cumberland, above the fells of Borrowdale.

Stainforth-under-Baergh (its old and correct name) came unto being above the stony ford of the Ribble, on the banks of a boulder-strewn brook, and below the limestone wall of Winskill Scar. So many ways converge upon it—the steps of the Winskill Giant are a slippery staircase of limestone down the tree-clad face of the Scar—the stony lane descends from Catterick and the Force in its deep ravine—a hillroad comes down from Malham Tarn and joins another from Silverdale and Peter Castle—and older than the highway which it leaves just beyond the village school, is the lane to Stainforth Bridge and the Foss.

No one ever planned a village like this. It just evolved—cottages perched by the stream, they took root on rocky platforms, they clustered where something was going on, by the stepping stones and the bridge, they grouped themselves at the beginning of paths and lanes along which the villagers drove out their flocks and herds.

HORTON-IN-RIBBLESDALE

Unlike Stainforth, Horton has an ancient church as focal point. In spite of this its lanes wriggle around and cottages are sited haphazardly, not only around churchyard, inns and grouped at bridges, but hidden down a labyrinth of elusive back lanes.

One lane pulls you up at the lychgate. There is the church, with its old lead roof looking so new that the uninformed remark, " What a pity—a tin roof ! " In fact it pre-dates the warring years and troubled times of Reformation and Civil War, when churches on

Lychgate, Horton Church

main travel routes were stripped of their lead and only out-of-the-way churches like this and Hubberholm's retained theirs.

Read the fine lettering of the eighteenth-century tombstones. Pass through the south door with its Norman arch, of simple chevron design, and notice how the builders of eight centuries ago cut the stone bowl of the font, shaped the arcading of the nave and attempted design on the pillar capitals.

One fragment of ancient stained-glass is interesting. It is the mitred head of Thomas à Becket whose murder was news when the church was young. On the glass are the words " Thomas Cantaur ".

At Horton, ardent walkers with rucksacks and maps discuss plans; some for walking across mountains, some for fell rambles; some are off on The Pennine Way, a wooden sign with these words upon it putting Horton firmly on the route from Edale to the Border.

It has always been a favourite starting point for me when off to the dales, being a stop (not enough trains do stop) on the Manchester-Blackburn-Hellifield-Garsdale line. Its station is an eye-opener, being a flower garden, information bureau on matters of altitude and latitude, climate, distances, a rest-room—with easy chairs, reading-room, art gallery and exhibition hall. From the window as you watch the rain streaming down, Penyghent stares across the dale at you, scoffing and pulling down a grey cloud-cap.

When the cloud wrack does lift, then away go the walkers, the climbers, amblers and scramblers. There are paths and tracks for all.

One, long distance, takes the green lane west of the mountain—starting out for New Houses and Scale, rounding the northern end of Penyghent and crossing the Pennine watershed to descend with Greenfield Beck to Beckermonds, Langstrothdale and the Wharfe at Buckden. A clear track all the way and hardly a soul in the vast landscape.

Another route, this time into Wensleydale, starts out on the same green lane to Scales but there strikes the track to Birkwith, Old Ings and the potholes of Cave Hill. This continues to Ling Gill, crosses Cam Beck by an old bridge, and therefrom climbs to the Roman way on Cam and follows it all the way into Bardale, Wether Fell, above Semerwater to Bainbridge.

Most dramatic scenery lies within and about Ling Gill, on stormy days a savage place, fit hiding place for demons and trolls imported by our Norse forefathers. In midwinter icicles like organ pipes hang from the cliffs and the gill holds a terrifying silence. But summer! Then it is a faery place, enchanting; rowans and rock-held hollies catch the sun and ledges are gay with foxgloves, harebells and sheep-bit scabious, and the air is loud with singing birds.

The bridge was built for the benefit of travellers on the main pre-turnpike road from Settle to Hawes, who had to struggle over The Cam and down Sleddale, whilst the Roman Road carried others bound for Bainbridge, Askrigg and the northern dales. Once they called this the Devil's Causeway—believing no human hands could have engineered such a road so well, enduring so long.

Long ago, men feared the onset of night on The Cam. They hastened onwards and glad they were when the sound of Bainbridge's horn was carried to them on the wind. Wolves ranged the tops; in the Middle Ages the hornblower sounded the alarm and a warning for all to bring down flocks and herds to safety.

Go forward now without fear from Cam Bridge, a mile of rough track, then on the wide ribbon of Roman way—green against the bronze and brown of the fell herbage—until two miles farther on the remote farm of Cam Houses appears, in a lonely dip. The watershed of England is not far beyond, near a small outbarn.

There, among insignificant rills rising among the rough tussocks, are the headsprings of two fair streams—a patch of felltop dividing them—the Wharfe is one, and the little runnel, narrow enough to stand astride—the Ribble itself, or, to avoid controversy, shall we say " one of its twin beginnings "?

And nothing could be lonelier, or wilder.

TO RIBBLEHEAD

From Horton, under the bleak foothills of Ingleborough, the bare slopes of Simon and Park Fell, there seems nothing to waylay us, only forbidding prospects. But leave the road; above the steep pastures of Selside is Alum Pot, one of the wonders of Craven, and mountain tracks penetrating into spectacular places—by Borrins and over limestone pavements to Sulber Nick and the cradled calm of Crummackdale, or heading for Simon Fell and Ingleborough's summit. Two miles north of Selside are two surprising off-the-road discoveries—one the old farm called Lodge Farm, or Ingman Lodge, which bears the airs and graces of a more opulent age, with history going back to monastic days, and the other a staggering blow for anyone who believes this to be an almost desert region devoid of trees and flowers.

Craven has areas protected for their natural and geological interest much as abbey and castles are scheduled for protection as ancient monuments. But Man never had any hand in the rock gardening and sensational landscaping of Colt Park—only half a mile from the highway. Norber above Austwick is a geological " parkland "; Colt Park is a paradise for botanists too, a lost roothold of rarities and not to be visited by any who cannot look, enjoy, study—and leave alone.

Have you ever attempted to leave the train at Ribblehead station on a stormy day? No station has a lonelier setting, so ringed around by lofty mountains, so much at the mercy of the elements. Heavy goods trains rumble by; only rarely do trains stop, but this does not mean that the station master has time on his hands. He scans the skies, he sends up balloons to assess cloud levels, he records the wind's velocity and weather changes, sending hourly messages to the "Met" Office, which in turn passes on the information to the air lines, " civil aviation control ".

With the first onslaught of Winter, Ribblehead is first in the news. Snowploughs are always at the ready. Life ceases to flow when snow storms block the roads and the railway line over this Roof of England. It was always so, to eighteenth-century travellers "a seat of misery in a desert, the scene black and frightful" and a "dread region where one felt a kind of inhospitable terror".

Ninety years ago when a "town" of hutments grew up on Batty Moss, the tough labourers and navvies who lived here, wintering and summering on the roof of England until a great railway line was completed, called it Siberia. Nowhere during their railway building experiences in many parts of the world had they struck such rigorous conditions as—at Ribblehead.

Often we have plodded through snow here when down in the valley there has been none. Of 1947—"that worst of winters"—a good story is often told about Ribblehead; a baker's van was caught in the drifts and left unprotected by the driver.

Corn in Egypt to a breadless, provisionless world! Farmers cut their way to the van, helped themselves to the loaves, carefully noted down their "purchases", and when the great eight weeks and three days' snow season ended and the van retrieved, the baker received payment to the last penny to account for all his load!

Snow at Easter is common enough. But how exhilarating those first clear breezy days of early spring, such as that of which Ruskin wrote. He stood leaning against the wind one April morning; he gazed at the dramatic ring of mountains—The Cam, Penyghent, Whernside—and felt "a vague sense of wonder" as he watched Ingleborough stand without rocking.

"There is not a square mile in the Settle district that we might not make a lifelong study of"; a local worthy is reported to have stated, and the author of a prosy Victorian "Rambles Round Settle" said he hoped this was "no extravagant hyperbole". You must be a walker to prove this is still no extravagance of statement; road travelling only hints at what is possible.

Among the "top ten" walks in the north-west this is my choice, best taken in two stages, west and east of Settle if day walking, the entire route; Kilnsey Crag in Wharfedale to Ingleton is for a weekend out of doors. Distance—12 to 14 miles in each direction.

Going west from Settle bridge; path to Stackhouse, fell track to Feizor, rough track or green packhorse route (choked by flowers in Summer) to Austwick, Thwaite Lane to Clapham, and the old highway near to Ingleborough foot, to Ingleton. After this there possibly is energy enough left to see the glens and falls by evening light.

Going east from Settle; stride out up Old Settle to Stockdale (and a digression to overlook Scaleber Foss) then by the dwindling lane and grassy track to Cove Road and the Cove's upper rim above Malhamdale. Then east from the village to Gordale—to view that "savage lair" of Gordale Scar—and forward by Lee Gate to the Mastiles Lane—Roman, medieval, drove road and a breezy route for us—before dropping to Kilnsey and the Wharfe.

An alternative, north of and parallel to the above, is to start from Constitution Hill, climb the green paths over Great High Fell to the rock ramparts of Attermire, cross country to Winskill farm and view Catterick Force beyond. Then strike fell paths east to the Malham Tarn road. After which forward over Mastiles.

Three Craven Mountains

CLIMBING INGLEBOROUGH

The leonine head of Ingleborough is an old friend recognized from many a lesser hilltop. The "far grey north regarding" it has the inscrutability of a sphinx. I think it is best loved of all our Pennine giants.

We look at it, climb it from Crina Bottoms or Trow Gill and Gaping Gill, and from its bald head survey the northern scene as proud as Cortez on his "peak in Darien".

Two centuries ago men assessed its height at nearly five miles high and the more conservative "the perpendicular height above the level of the sea 2,967 feet", which was not so far out.

Tourists began to climb it for fun in the eighteenth century "and received much amusement from viewing several extensive and diversified prospects and in making observations as botanists and historians". Otherwise only shepherds and "local countryfolk who resorted to the horse races formerly held annually on its summit" ever toiled upwards.

Some professed to identify a stone pile as relic of a beacon; others the wall around the mile-long perimeter as defences of a Roman station. Celtic hill defenders had their look-outs on top and Iron Age tribesmen stockaded camps along the hill foot. Anglian ploughlands, some a thousand years old, pattern the slopes above Clapham and Newby; Norse hill farms surround the mountain and their names predominate for hamlets and natural features, for the caves and potholes which proved so fascinating to these believers in trolls, evil spirits, demons pent in underground prisons, and underworld gods.

Only one mark of modern times; the cruciform Coronation shelter on the summit, where as the mists come down wanderers wait and hope for the blanket to be torn apart, or climbers seek respite from howling gales.

Two farms only share the immensity of the mountain, built long ago out of the very bones and sinews of Ingleborough, on its rock, of its rock—Crina farm and Clapdale. How dramatic their sites, the first in amazing emerald intakes cleared by what herculean efforts from rocks and boulders which were piled to make its walls, the second like a rock-built fortress at the edge of secret ravines.

If you start out from Clapham you can climb the stony "gooseberry lane" to Clapdale or, paying a few coppers at the Saw Mill Cottage, take the private drive through Ingleborough Hall grounds, dim mysterious glades above beck and lake, into the same secret valley. The last habitation is Clapdale Hall, ancestral home of Claphams, where the scene is much as it always was. Alpine pastures

" Lion-fronted " Ingleborough

around it, farming activity going on, hay-timing, sheep-clipping and marking in June—the sheep mark is a "red stroke on the near side".

The dale floor is the greenest of greensward, the beck crystal clear as it chuckles, "clapping its stones together"; from the thorns, you hear the sarcastic yaffling of the green woodpecker, the shout of the cuckoo. A place innocent of drama? But wait; the portals of Ingleborough Cave are just ahead, ready to swallow up the droves of cave explorers and beyond again, away from the noise of underground waters emerging to rush over rocks, a pregnant silence. The dale narrows, the rocks draw nearer, the walls loom higher and you are in the dim shades of Trow Gill.

A place of shudders and shivers; the sun never penetrates, nor do any birds but the raven or carrion crow dare to croak. Only our own footsteps, a rolling stone, a snapped twig, break the dead quiet.

No place to linger. Scrambling to the shut-in upper end of the Gill we find a rock-strewn path, a gap, and we are out in a world of sunshine, a dazzle of light, with harebells fluttering by the wall, white butterflies, and curlews calling. The nailed boots of walkers have scratched and smoothed the stones of the path to a stile, making the way clear to the brink of Gaping Gill.

I am fearful of yawning abysses like this and keep well back. It was thought to be a bottomless pit until John Birkbeck of Settle in the 1840s and Martel the Frenchman in 1895 were lowered into its depths. Now the potholing clubs have "open days", bring along their winding gear and the adventuresome are lowered—and brought up again—in safety.

Gaping Gill is one of the wonders of the north. Around 360 feet deep, it could contain a cathedral in its depths. The underground system is extensive enough to keep potholers busy for years—and it has not yet yielded all its secrets.

The path climbs towards Little Ingleborough, squelching over spongy ground where sphagnum moss holds the moisture and rushes grow luxuriantly in runnels.

A stiffer climb follows over screes and boulder spills, the hard gritstone platform of Little Ingleborough; up again, and after a final scramble the undoubted mountain top with nothing but the sky above.

This is the easy way up, far less steep than the more dramatic climb from Crina Bottoms, up the groove once dubbed The Devil's Pass.

Are you puffed? Then you must appreciate what Robert Balderston wrote in 1830.

"How often does the weary toiler when wending up the steeps, think that his plodding steps will have brought him to the goal when the slope he is ascending has been surmounted! How often does his astonished eye find yet another ridge beyond. At last a steepier, rockier girdle is found above the mountain brow, spangled with lines of millstone grit—a ducal coronet as bands of strawberry leaves crowning the noble head."

This is it, the top, where he can lay down his weary limbs for a while. Then suddenly he finds he is a new man. What does he do?

"He finds a sudden vigour—the keen mountain air's wonderful recuperative spell has done its work, and springing to his feet with elastic step and new-born buoyancy he casts his eye around."

We all taste this mountain elixir, headier than champagne, and feeling on top of the world in more ways than one, "cast our eyes around".

The first ring of mountains includes those almost Ingleborough's equals, Greygarth, Great Coum, and Whernside, his superior, Penyghent, The Cam, Widdale Fell and far to the east the long blue ridge of Fountains Fell.

Lancastrians look south to find the familiar whaleback hulk of Pendle. Mountain lovers search the north-western skyline to see the Westmorland fells, the Cumbrian giants, the peaks and pikes which pile up beyond the shining levels of Morecambe Bay. Some claim they can trace the outline of the Isle of Man, riding the Irish Sea.

And some, alas, see nothing at all but wait patiently till the clouds lift and the track back to Ingleton is revealed.

Mountains are great levellers. Everyone talks to everyone else. We talk to two keen climbing types, of the hard way up from Hill Inn and Chapel-le-Dale; they say they "looked-in" at the Great Douk and Little Douk caves and found more pasture edge potholes "promising".

A family party appears, a six-year-old first scrambling up the giant terraces and the Devil's Pass; Mother arrives last, hot but smiling, delighted at her own achievement.

A rambling club next, in twos and threes; a Manchester "ramblers" special train dropped them at Horton. They had climbed from Alum Pot and Simon's Fell.

No Three Peakers among them.

To be a Three Peaker you must be able to cover great distances and climb the three Craven mountains in succession, and in one day. This calls for some stamina, though the two masters of Giggleswick School who pioneered the walk in 1887—a June day after school was over—completed the circuit in their stride.

The shortest distance to link the Ingleborough, Penyghent and Whernside cairns is twenty-one miles. Energetic walkers, counting their progress as leisurely, walk the three in twelve hours. Runners starting out from Hill Inn, up Whernside and down to Ribblehead, up Penyghent and down to Horton, up Ingleborough and haring it back to Hill Inn, have "'run" it in five hours!

Mountain lovers can ignore all this and feel no shame. My own preference is for one peak, one day. Let the winners of the Ingleborough Mouutain Race strain to reduce their up and down timing below fifty-five minutes. Let the hares leap the tops. I will be with the tortoise stopping and staring, taking all in and needing a full summer's day to do it in.

Two centuries ago when very curious travellers ranged the length and breadth of Ingleborough searching for potholes they had no code for behaviour on mountains.

One wrote of looking down Alan or Alum Pot near Selside, " a terrible hiatus into which a cascade dropped causing such a dreadful gloom from the spray to make us shrink back with horror ". It was protected only by a low mound of earth " for a stone wall would serve no other useful purpose than to afford the traveller materials to throw in for his amusement ".

No chucking stones down potholes! Some years ago someone carelessly dropped a stone down Alum Pot. It killed a woman pot-holer down the shaft.

Rehearse these rules with youngsters new to mountains.

Stones, and what NOT to do with them.

Never, never, throw stones down holes or potholes.

Never send rocks hurtling, or stones bouncing, down slopes, for it needs but one rolling stone to set a whole rocky fellside slipping, and one stone, gathering momentum, might injure a walker, or kill a sheep.

Never pull down the stones of a wall in climbing, but if any are dislodged, replace them, otherwise flocks may stray.

An H.M.I. putting a class of farmer's children through their arith-metic was put to rights over a matter of straying sheep.

" There were a hundred sheep in a field and twenty-six found a gap in the wall. How many were left? "

" None, sir," replied one lad without hesitation.

True, but not the answer the Inspector wanted.

ON AND AROUND PENYGHENT

> " From Penyghent's proud foot, as from my source I slide,
> That mountain my proud sire, in height of all his pride,
> Takes pleasure in my course, as in his first-born flood."

So spake Ribble in Drayton's poem, ignoring the claims of Whern-side. But Penyghent is so much more pushing and aggressive, domina-ting the upper dale.

What a fine Welsh-sounding name it has—maybe Pen-y-Gwynt, hill of the winds, or " haply so called of its white and snowy top for so Pengwyn signifies in the old Welsh tongue ". More modern place-name experts say it is Pen-y-Gaint, meaning open country.

It is all of the three—in turn, and all at once.

Try climbing the mountain on a day when the wild north-easters race across Penyghent Gill; it will blow you up and give you no time to poise on the top before it pushes you down again. Or, leaving Horton on a balmy summer day when soft airs play in the green lanes as far as Hull Pot, turn up to the "slack of the hill" the hollow back of the monster, and very soon stronger breezes go with you and leave you leaning helplessly against a stone pile, holding on to all you have.

Its bald crown is the first to be whitened by winter snow, and its gullies the last to lose the white streaks left from snowdrifts. The farms of Penyghent Gill are among the first to feel the rigours of blizzards and are constantly in a state of siege against the elements.

Penyghent's proud head

Open country; miles of it, with never a tree to break the raking slopes. Try to find shelter east side or west. The drystone walls which divide vast "allotments" are built to allow the wind to pass through their chinks instead of battering them down. Hark at the whistling wind in the crannies!

Having come into Ribblesdale from Lancashire it is likely the climb will be made from Horton-in-Ribblesdale on its west side, or from the Settle, Stainforth to Halton Gill motor road on its east.

From Horton a rough, walled-in lane with the exciting Dowgill on its right hand, rises gradually in 2 miles to the gate at Hull Pot. This tremendous cavity, "like the inside of a great Gothic castle, the high ruinous walls of which were left standing after the roof had fallen in, " is one of the many wonders along Penyghent foot.

Turning right and through another fell gate, keeping straight on to the saddle and we have completed the 4 mile walk from Horton. Once up we can open our arms to the wind and exult in it and, climbing the "lion's mane", stagger up to the top cairn, the tuft on its bald head. The gritstone crags fall sheer to the south, screes run down to the lonely pastures and one wall seems to lead direct to Churn Milk Hole, Dale Head, Peter Castle. Thin dark walls define an old track far away and below; that is the lane which takes us south to Helwith Bridge and the Ribble again, part of the same fell route we can see over to the east struggling out of Penyghent Gill—once a high-level pack-horse way from the north.

Although views from Penyghent are not so extensive as from the two higher peaks there is an intimacy about them I love. Littondale is a gentle green Eden, its fell walls like a Viking ship—the Skirfare a thin thread along its floor, and a happy sight, the scattered farms, especially in hay time when their fields are a chequerboard of gold, greens dark and light. Ribblesdale, too, is a land of patchwork meadow, small intakes and high fell side "allotments"—and white plumes of smoke from the passing trains heading towards Ribble-head and the Blea Moor wasteland. We look over the hunting country where the Cliffords once took their pleasure and over the Fountains Abbey sheepwalks on the fell they named, from which the monks derived so much wealth when riches lay in fleeces.

A kestrel hovers higher than our mountain top; he falls swiftly towards one tiny tarn not far from Hunt Pot and we lose him in a welter of boulders.

Following the crumbling wall down the "lion's mane", we come to the saddle again, between head and haunches, and down goes the way over spongy turf, avoiding boggy places, coming to the side of a merry little beck, a guide down to the grey road not far from Penyghent Gill farm.

This is the simplest ascent for any who bring their cars up from Settle and Stainforth into Silverdale. Reaching Dale Head gate they carry on past the Rainscar House, with fine beef cattle in its pastures, coming to the watershed and the upper end of a deep gill. A lovely picnic spot—a little bridge, the babbling beck, cushioned seats; turf and heather—and Penyghent inviting. You cannot resist it.

PERAMBULATING PENYGHENT

It is a pity so few trains stop at Horton-in-Ribblesdale station, for the railway staff has been going all out to beautify the platform, with commendable results. Very few passengers have time to read the information displayed for their benefit as trains rush by—to learn that Horton has a population of 700, an altitude of 850 feet, is in Yorkshire West Riding, has Carlisle 65 miles north of it and London 242 miles to the south, along the line. There is a fine shield-of-arms of the Riding, the motto, all carefully painted. Stocks and marigolds and a colourful border of flowers stretch on both platforms. From this station go forth potholers to descend, mountaineers to climb, and fell walkers to perambulate Penyghent—as we did.

A green drove road of great age climbs from Helwith Bridge (south of Horton) to Dale Head and Hesleden beyond the mountain. To avoid a long walk to the old road, we cut up steep pastures, crossed fields where hay had been mown or "piked", and, reaching Newlands farm, were directed the best way to Long Lane, out of sight over the skyline.

The way was steep, but the breeze was cool, and there was good reason to pause a dozen times to admire the Ribblesdale landscape There was dramatic cloudplay over Ingleborough, a scowl of cloud over farther Whernside, a curtain of rain was travelling quickly before a swift wind, whilst a funnel of rain appeared to be emptying about Ribblehead.

Eventually we "hit the trail", the Long Lane from Helwith which climbed to Churn Milk Hole, a deep bowl at the track edge. We came in turn to Dale Head farm, which lies at the upper end of Silverdale, a valley which goes down to Stainforth—to Rainscar farm, where men were leading hay from high-flung meadows—over Blishmire Close, where we began to glimpse northwards the guardian fells of Littondale—over rough land where Bronze Age hillmen buried their dead in a "Giants' Grave"—and so to the bridge near Penyghent House.

In monastic times great abbeys owned vast sheep-walks over these fells; in earlier times native herdsmen pastured their flocks on the slopes above the deep ravine and contrived folds with walls of riven limestone to protect them against wolves.

The grey road goes on to Halton Gill and into Littondale, dropping from the heights to the green and peaceful valley, where loveliness is cradled among bare steeps and gleaming scars. We leave the road to take a short cut over The Berghs (pronounced "barks") to Foxup.

But short cuts on fell land do not always prove quickest progress. The best paths we found were sheep trods. There were high and awkward walls to climb. We could see the trim compact group of houses which comprise Halton Gill, far below us; we traced the zig-zags of Horse Head pass, the drove road from Helwith Bridge to Dale Head, to Raisgill, Oughtershaw and Hawes.

A high wind swept over The Berghs, this time bringing swift-closing curtains of rain. Heifers in the pasture ran for shelter to a distant wall. We crouched against a boulder, heard the pelting rain, watched Littondale disappear. A few minutes—the sun came through, the rain was over, two rainbows trembled over the valley, linking fell and fell with an enchanted bridge. Sunlight glinted on streaming rocks, on wet grasses—and on the nose-ring of a bull not many yards behind us.

One cannot dispute rights of way with a bull. We eyed him, veered silently away from him—and he turned away to his grazing. We breathed again.

From Foxup to Hull Pot is a long 4 miles along a path which goes from gate to gate through six or seven vast pastures, closes and intakes, each one stretching from Plover Fell to Foxup beck-bottom —across wild country which can have changed very little in a thousand years. When Foxup had disappeared below the lower slopes, we looked about and saw nothing of man's handiwork—only mountain, bog, heather, only fells near and far and the sky with an occasional curlew.

At Hull Pot—a long rift at the fell end, where the green road, walled-in to Horton, begins, we saw walkers again and joined them to catch the same "ramblers' train" home.

THE MOUNTAIN CALLED WHERNSIDE

Said a walking enthusiast, lover of wide open spaces and loneli-ness, "Whernside is best of the lot. You can get away from crowds up there. Hardly ever see a soul." His finger pointed out his route on a battered map. From Ingleton, escape from the highway, a farm track going in turn past the farms of Beezeleys, Dale Barn and into Chapel-le-Dale, then to Philpin, Gunnerfleets and that remote farm gripped between mountains, Winterscales.

"Reminds me of Norway, all these names."

The country around here is heavily overlaid with names given by our Norse forbears, all bestowed nearly a thousand years ago when Viking settlers thought all this looked very much like home. The Angles ignored these high dales, preferring richer acres in regions less isolated, but it was fitting ground for hardy Norsemen, who came here, summering and wintering, building their "scales" or bothies far into the fells.

So, if you want to know the joys of complete isolation from the outer world make for Ribblehead, by road or parallel tracks, heading for Winterscales and go forward with valiant heart into the wilds.

One note, discordant or welcome, depending on the attitude you have towards trains, occasionally rends the air. The Carlisle line is a close companion far into Blea Moor, into which it disappears for almost 2 miles.

After a solitary day on the fells I find the train a welcome sight and hear the engine whistle with no more feeling of it being out of keeping than I would a curlew's cry.

I like to see it "lap the miles and lick the valleys up", and roar across the landscape, "shovelling white steam over its shoulder".

A century ago the wilderness about the Batty Moss viaduct was noisy with railway building and tough gangs of navvies. Two centuries ago thousands of head of cattle lowed and tossed their heads when Newby Moor and Gearstones were places of Autumn marts. Apart from navvies and drovers few came here and the old routes over Whernside were only known to colliers who worked on Greensett and Coal Gill and millstone getters, who hewed the rock from the mountain's cap.

Few would guess it, but the wide green track which sweeps over Whernside's shoulder is an ancient road known as Craven's Old Way and a short cut into Dentdale. Eighteenth-century travellers knew it, and Scots drovers hastening north again after selling their cattle, and the odd and goggle-eyed curious travellers venturing hither on their Tour of the Caves of Yorkshire.

"The prospects were not diversified by many pleasing objects, being surrounded on almost all sides with brown and blue chaotic mountains," wrote one.

He had climbed, as walkers do today, from Winterscales, beside the dwindling streams, up the steep slope, over boggy ground, then along the foot of Greenside Craggs and Hagg Worm Haws, following the green road until Cable Rake tempted him to the mountain top.

It is more likely that modern travellers reaching Dentdale by road will climb from that northern side. A favourite walk begins at the back door of Deeside House, the youth hostel, which was once a shooting box of the Cavendish-Bentincks.

It begins at the mountain foot, passes from lower pastures to take in a shooters' path, climbing with Blake Gill to its fountain head. Green intakes and deep gills from which the tops of rowans peep— they are left behind; so are cascading becks and the heathery slopes.

We walk on a limestone plateau, on water-smoothed slabs between which are cushions of wild thyme or small ferns in crannies. At the rock margin crystal fountains, liquid air, bubble away. There are scores of these springs and all are named. Follow Craven's Old Way and in turn we pass and refresh ourselves, as man and beast have done down the years, at Birk Pot, Horse Well, Old Wife's Well, and

How Gill, Boot Sike and Thorough Mea Springs, Fish Sike or Fold Well. Homely names for such enchanting wayside fountains.

There is a shooting hut where sheep eye the rambler blandly, then a level terrace, a line of "shakeholes", some named, some nameless, into which disappear the waters which are to re-appear as the named springs by the green road. North of the shakeholes appear signs of coal workings. Millstone Hill is higher still, site of the quern and grindstone workshops, much used when local mills were grinding corn and sharpening blades on Whernside's stone.

And here are the three tarns and the silent Men of Whernside, guardians of a charmed peace. Here we linger longest, watching the dreaming waters draw into them the deepest blue in the heavens.

Whernside from Craven's Old Way

Perchance you think the tops have a permanent male population; let it be known that the Men are cairns, "maen" being Celtic for stone piles.

May is the time when bird lovers climb to the Tarns. Then you might think snowdrifts remained, unthawed, from Winter. About the shores is whiteness whiter than the silversand. When an intruder draws near there is a warning call; then whiteness breaks up and becomes a flight of gulls. Thousands come here at nesting time, to this, a favourite breeding ground.

Let the silversand about the tarn edge trickle through your fingers. This was sought for by dales' farmers when they whetted their scythes and sickles on "honing stickles" made in the simplest way; they covered the stick with sheep's fat then rolled it in the silversand. The sand was utilized also down at the marble mills at Arten

Gill, where the local dark limestone was polished to a mirror-like smoothness.

There are no mountains in the Pennines quite like the swarthy beasts which crouch above the Lune valley at Howgill and which turn their heads to glower on Whernside. These Westmorland fells join the family of giants we have looked upon from the other Craven tops; they lead the eye to the Lakeland skyline.

"Brown and blue chaotic mountains," wrote one.

"God, what anatomy, what beauty! What superb, bald beasts they are!" wrote another, and he not an Englishman.

For admiring mountains, "Whernside beats all!"

Descend as you wish, to Dentdale head, or down the green road to Deepdale and Dent's Town, or strike towards Deepdale head and the fell road to Kingsdale and Ingleton.

One warning; a go-as-you-please route occasionally ends in an argument with a bull.

ROAD ROUTES

While roamers ramble and climbers strain to the heights, what is the car owner to do?

For them are mountain circuits and, as "love of mountains is an acquired habit—and there are those who like to gaze on them from a safe distance", I suggest the following routes. O.S. Sheet 90 helps.

Ingleborough Roundabout; from Settle, up Buckhaw Brow, take the old coaching road signposted "Feizor" for wider views, and descend again through Austwick and on to Clapham, taking the higher road by Yarlsber to Ingleton. Take the road north through Chapel-le-Dale to Ribblehead, returning to Settle by Horton and Stainforth. (26 miles.)

Encircling Penyghent; this involves a wide sweep from Settle to Ribblehead and Hawes, a climb from Wensleydale, by Sleddale, to Bardale Head and Fleet Moss (wonderful views down to Semerdale) and the long road down Langstrothdale to Hubberholm, and down Wharfedale to Kettlewell. At Skirfare Bridge roads run into Litton-dale, where Penyghent at the dale head comes into the picture. Beyond Arncliffe a stiff and tortuous fell road goes over to Malham Tarn, but the road up Penyghent Gill to Peter Castle and Stainforth strikes towards the mountain foot, along its eastern side, beyond Litton. This route, 52 miles, is for experienced drivers with explora-tory instincts. None of these fell routes are for inexperienced motorists.

All round Whernside; another fell route definitely not for the inexperienced driver or for any car containing timorous passengers.

For others it is a most exhilarating run with some sensational descents and breath-taking views.

Leave Ingleton for Thornton-in-Lonsdale, there setting out along the Kingsdale road above the glens and waterfalls into a quiet valley once thought fit only for "hermit and anchorite". Above the last dale head farm comes a hairpin rise, up and up, to the skyline on White Shaw Moss and, poising a moment, down we go more suddenly into the depths of Deepdale. Plenty of time, however, to admire Whernside and enjoy the unfolding of the Dentdale landscape. A break of journey in Dent's Town, then updale through Cowgill and Lea Gate to Dent Head. Beyond the railway viaduct is Wold Fell, which gives birth to the infant Ribble. We have the river growing in size and strength, as companion all the way to Ribblehead. To keep Whernside in sight we travel down to Ingleton by Chapel-le-Dale. (25 miles.)

TWO

PENDLE AND THE CALDER COUNTRY

Pendle from Fish Moor

I Pendle

The Hill—a Portrait

" Penighent, Pendle hill, Ingleborough,
   Three such hills be not all England through.
   I long to climbe up Pendle; Pendle stands
   Rownd cop, survaying all ye wilde moorelands—"

THAT WAS PENDLE as Richard James thought of it in 1636 during his tour of Lancashire, when the hill was very much headline news following two trials of notorious local witches.

Whether his wish to climb Pendle was realized I do not know. Probably like many others of his time he looked upon it from afar, appraised it, and repeated the couplet which in various forms puts our Lancashire hill among the Craven giants. Years before, Camden quoted a local rhyme—

" Ingleborrow, Pendle Hill and Penighent
   Bee the highest hills between Scotland and Trent ",

and in the eighteenth century Daniel Defoe was naming Pendle in the trio of mountains " monstrous high ", in a countryside " all

mountainous and full of innumerable high hills it was not easy for
a traveller to judge which was highest".

That was when topographers thought the Pennines were Everest-
high. Pendle, in fact, misses mountain status by 169 feet—but every
inch is used to such good effect that it has pride of place now, as
then, among all the sky-reaching heights seen from the Lancashire
towns.

Affection and familiarity put Old Pendle high in our esteem.
Our Ancient British forbears spoke of it as The Hill—Pen in the
Celtic tongue—worshipping their deities upon its summit. The
Romans marching along its flanks knew it by the same name, and
when the Angles came upon it from the north in the seventh
century they merely added their own form of hill name so that it
became Penull.

The hill is the local weather glass:

Camden said that Pendle gives certain signs of rain "whenever
its summit is covered with clouds". A true saying which is repeated
in various forms today.

> "If Pendle's head do wear a hood
> Be sure the day will ne'er do good."

The farmer looking out during haytime and seeing cloud wrack
in the Pendle gullies says, "I might as well go back to bed. It will
never make a hay-day." And the converse is also true; if the hill is
clear of clouds at daylight the day is always good. I know—I look
every morning from my bedroom window.

In stature Pendle is a lowly hill, but when we have watched
from its summit the passing of a midsummer night and the coming
to life of a midsummer morning with the aubades of curlew and
rising lark, then we have felt very near to the gates of Heaven.
With daylight flooding across a sleeping world, on the hill is

> "—eternity made manifest
> With dignity of timeless years".

Because of George Fox, the founder of their sect, Quakers climb
Pendle in the spirit of pilgrimage, following the route he climbed
in the Spring of 1652. With his journal in hand they read his words
and meditate.

> "We came near a very high hill, called Pendle Hill and I was
> moved of the Lord to go to the top of it; which I did with much
> ado, it was so very steep and high. When I was come to the top
> I saw the sea bordering upon Lancashire. From the top of this hill
> the Lord let me see in what places he had a great people to be

gathered. As I went down I found a spring of water in the side of the hill, with which I refreshed myself—"

The spring is there now, Fox's Well.

Folk living around Pendle toil to the hilltop to watch the Midsummer sunrise, continuing without knowing it a custom begun when their forefathers were sun worshippers—or so traditionalists like to think. Mostly the young folk arrange such nights out. I have watched dawn on the hill and the glory of the late setting of the sun on Midsummer Eve, and both are memorable experiences.

Pendle West Side Byways

Byways are best north of Whalley. Pig Cottage (pretty flagged garden and a "pig", which is more likely a badger, over its door) is at the Wiswell road end, pointing the way to Pendleton, the Nick of Pendle, Worston and Downham.

It is as narrow and tortuous as signs give warning, trees all along framing pleasant panoramas. Pendle and the moors stretch on one hand, the Ribble Valley with Clitheroe Castle riding high over the grey rooftops of the old borough, Longridge and its Red Indian profile, and the blue Bowland hills on the other.

En route, take note of Wiswell Shay cross, new shaft on its ancient base, a mile from church and abbey, the spot where funeral cortèges out of Pendle Forest and worshippers heading for Whalley used to pause, intone their dirges or pray.

Wiswell Hall farm, unremarkable today, is on the site of the Tudor homestead of the Paslews, a son of the family, a bright boy, becoming the last abbot of Whalley; many a tradition about him still lingers hereabouts.

Wiswell village is pleasant; Vicarage farm is a good, well-modernized example of the typical seventeenth-century yeoman's house. The inn hides away down a back lane and the village trough is overhung by a chestnut of umbrella-like proportions.

Any place with a name like Cold Cotes, signifying buildings cast out on a bare hillside "cold as charity", you must expect to be sited high. A mile on, our Cold Cotes has shelter now of many trees, but we can guess what it was like five centuries ago when the Walmsleys lived here in their Hall built around a courtyard. From its rear gate a path by Hagley Clough and the old Hunting Gate comes to an ancient community far more remote, far more at the mercy of the elements, Whymondhouses.

I think Pendleton is much as we expect an English village to be, farms, cottages and substantial old houses lined up on both banks of a brook, ducks dabbling, geese patrolling and nothing but rural sounds to disturb the light sleep into which, after a long and busy life, it has lapsed. Like the best villages it is "mixed", the bright new Institute near the Swan With Two Necks, the Victorian houses and Jacobean cottages and Georgian mansion all fitting in.

THE NICK OF PENDLE

Names like this, and Walloper Well, Trough of Bowland, Buck-haw Brow, have a thrill for northern countrylovers. But what do strangers expect to find at The Nick?

Not the Wellsprings, once a humble, five-day-licence inn, haunt of market-bound farmers, drovers, and in early days of packhorse drivers and chapmen, as a modern roadhouse where soft-footed orientals pad around and anyone so desiring can be served with chop suey.

Bomb Disposal notices are something of a shock too—but soon the hill will be cleared of dangerous wartime missiles and hill walkers once again able to roam, free as the wind.

When men trod out new tracks across country in prehistoric times they took their bearings from unmovable landmarks—rocks, peaks—and made on skylines "sighting cuttings". I like to think the nick or notch on the saddle between the fells and Pendle proper, was so made, and that the ancient hillway is part of that prehistoric Long Causeway linking the eastern and the western seas.

In historic times it was a route from Clitheroe into the Chase and Forest of Pendle—in medieval times a trading route—until turnpike roads and railways took over transport, a busy packhorse road.

> "Straight mine eye hath caught new pleasures
> Whilst the landscape round it measures,
> Russet lawns and fallows grey——".

Milton's poem comes to life when we stand on a clear day above The Nick. Climbing higher along the ridge above Ashenden Clough the view widens and lengthens; given a good following south-west wind you can be over the rough ground, striding towards the head of Ogden Clough and Mearley Clough like a ship with a gale in its tail, in three miles reaching Pendle's highest point, the cairn on the Big End.

Or, to escape too boisterous winds, take the stony track from the road gate in the hill gap, roll down to the cluster of farmhouses in the lee of the moors and see for yourself the kind of remote community where Lancashire nonconformity took roothold in the early days of Charles II. A vicar of Altham church, Thomas Jollie, being one of the thousands evicted from their churches in 1662, chose this lonely spot to gather together his congregation when the new laws forbade him to linger within five miles of his old living. Congregationalism was born at Whymondhouses in those years.

An exhilarating downhill spin, passing Pendleton Hall snug in its clough where the Hoghtons built it four centuries ago, and we are at Four Lane Ends where, an old uncle told me, his great-grandfather remembered a gibbet and the hanging of a sheep stealer.

The old highway heads for Clitheroe, but we turn to follow the lane to Worston.

TO WORSTON AND WORSA HILL

Pendle is with us all the way, with its breezy pastures cried over by curlews and peewits, and wind-bent thorns of great age. Many paths strike towards the hill, each one making for a Pendle foot farm.

A thousand years ago Anglian farmers with an eye on good well-drained limestone pastures, sweet herbage for their flocks and herds, chose to settle down in a green land among coral reef knolls. One was Crow Hill, joined by Ridge to Worsa Hill named after one of their leaders. So Worsa's Tun came into being. A little west of the settlement was a Roman highway; legionaries travelled it between Ribchester and York, but now as a grass-floored track gone back to Nature walkers in high Summer need protection from beds of nettles which choke it.

Ireland is not more emerald than the Worston landscape. Just wander along the brook through Worsa Bottoms as far as Worsa End farm, there to climb the thyme-carpeted slopes of the bare hill above it; an hour on its bald head, under a blue June sky—pure bliss! Much we see can have changed very little down the centuries.

Worston's "big house", the Hall, is now a farm. In Tudor days the manorial lords were the Greenacres but, the male line ending, their daughter's husband, Nicholas Assheton of Downham, in the early days of James I, came into possession of the estate, joining it to that of Downham. And so the two remain, as one. During altera-tions to the Hall, Greenacres acquired abbey stones from Sawley, then being demolished; three shields of arms they used to adorn the porch and more carved masonry, doorhead, archway and fluted pillar fragments are built into the garden wall.

Nicholas kept a journal of his activities, at home and away—and many of his entries were of events around Worston and the hill. For a taste—"June 24: to Worston Wood. Tried for a fox—took a rabbit. 25: Killed bitch fox in Warren (Worsa Hill). Caught and killed a badger on Salthill. 26: Fox in Worston Wood—to Bolton by Bowland. And on May 18: Worston. Coming home on Worsoe Fogg cried Fire in Warren House. Cuthbert Hearon the warrener with drying of gunpowder which fired the house." The diaries cover the years 1617-1618 and provide a lively picture of the way a Lancashire country squire of the period occupied his time.

Children enjoy scaring one another. There is a cottage in Worston, near the inn, with massive chimney, thick walls and a tiny round wheel window, which we used to insist was The Witch's House, hardly daring to look round when we passed for fear Old Mother Demdike was squinting out at us. Crow Hill Cottage is its name.

The Calf's Head is not what it was. Old pictures show it as a small, unpretentious village inn with stabling and farm included. In less sophisticated days the menfolk gathered under its roof and as excuse for jokes and ribaldry elected from their number Mayor and Corporation. Which was very well, until in excess of loyalty they tendered an address on a royal occasion and received a gracious acknowledgment from the Palace of St. James's. How was the Palace to know there was no place called Worston with civic status?

Behind the inn and the village street the brook flows through forget-me-nots and brooklime along the edge of the Green. In those old days which were not so good and men baited the bull for sport, saying beef tasted better after it, here Worston assembled en masse for Shrovetide diversions. The bullring needs some finding in a tangle of high grasses, but there it is, firmly held in its stone base.

CLIMBING PENDLE

Worston is the starting point for a frontal attack on the hill. Easiest is the climb through the Clough from Little Mearley Hall, a mile or so from the village.

The Hall is a gem, its setting on a level plot where a rushing stream calms down, after its descent in steps and ledges, is quite romantic. The Nowells had an eye for beauty, or were they merely thinking of the shelter woods and hillside offered them, and water unfailing, and vast pastures for their sheep, and rich meadowland to feed their kine? One of them, Christopher, brought here from the dismantled Sawley Abbey a very handsome bay window which was part of the abbot's dwelling. His initials and date are on the doorhead at the rear of the house.

Many is the time we have raced for shelter in a rainstorm to the giant sycamore by the farmyard watering troughs; there was always ample protection under its umbrella spread, and security its dense foliage provided.

The path goes through the sheepfolds; always activity here in June, marking, ear-clipping, tail-dockings of lusty lambs, and later shearing, washing, dippings—clamour, barking, bleating, baa-ing.

The way through the wood; uphill, gate to gate, away from the sun and cheerful farmyard noises, into a glade dappled with light and shade, the cascading stream alongside. The ravine cuts through many layers of Pendle grits and shales—interesting to geologists—which at different times have been subject to the all-powerful action of water-bursts.

The effect of a water-burst has to be seen to be believed. One

Little Mearley Hall

devastated valley walkers know well is near the Windermere Trout-beck, a hillside torn up, walls levelled, a dale floor strewn with rocks and boulders after a swift storm one June afternoon.

Pendle has its recorded "brasts" in 1580, 1669, and scores of lesser waterquakes have torn and gouged the hill slopes. The worst of them was responsible for the gash known as Brast Clough—which the writer of *Lancashire Witches* made the result of wizardry. A brast at Little Mearley strewed the flat fields with enough stones and debris to build the pasture walls; Plover Field is enclosed by walls of water-worn stones.

Now for the climb. Turn your back on the farm, take to the woods as far as the top gate. Pendle is waiting, a brooding monster. As you gaze it seems to stir slightly; is it going to stretch itself, yawn, wake and roar?

Go through the right-hand gate and there is a dipper-haunted pool, a waterfall and green overhanging branches often bright with spray. The left gate possibly has a warning—BULL : KEEP OUT—and whether you take it as false or true depends on your temerity. If in doubt, keep an eye on escape routes and be prepared to run for it. The odds are you will reach the ruined walls of the barn high up the slope and come to the vague diagonal track which becomes more clearly defined as you go forward; 2 miles from the farm you climb with a stone wall alongside to the top of the hill.

Pendle feels all of its 1,831 feet. The view is tremendous and especially dramatic westwards to the Bowland fells over the gentle Ribblesdale landscape, and northwards to the Craven mountains— true mountains being the full statutory height of 2,000 feet plus— though none of the superior trio, Ingleborough, Penyghent or Whernside, makes better use of its inches than Old Pendle.

The trio belong to Yorkshire. Pendle almost did; one of the streams cutting into its foothills northwards is the Yorkshire boundary and a farm near it bears the truly Yorkshire name of Craven Laithe. Ings Beck is a border stream passing just to the east of Twiston, a name which in its first form Twyssultune meant a village at the forking of boundary streams. The ancient borderline was between two Anglian kingdoms—Northumbria and Mercia.

The limits of the landscape—Craven, the Irish Sea with that much-sought-after landmark, Blackpool Tower, sticking up from the flat Fylde coastline, the Mersey estuary and the blue Welsh mountains. Eastwards roll the Pennines, with plenty of drama in their unfolding. Whether York Minster can be seen on one hand and Lancaster Castle on the other is highly controversial. A knowledgeable native climbed Pendle during the Festival of Britain when York was floodlit and, using powerful lenses, thought he picked out the Minster tower.

WORSTON TO DOWNHAM

The lane between the two is a bag of small delights, tender flowers in spring, honeysuckle and wild roses in summer, all the berries we expect of Autumn, and the red of holly berries for Christmas. Such small pleasures must be taken slowly. The road hog will soon be ditched, or worse. Twists and turns, deep ditches which are running water, high hedges hiding what lies ahead—that is the lane which finally sidles into Downham, shyly, as though it has no right to be there.

Early in 1961 this countryside came very much to life with all the activity and excitement of a film location. Imagine local interest with village schoolchildren acting crowd scenes and bright youngsters playing roles—and all their proud parents watching the unusual goings-on during the bright crisp days of February and March. Secretly the neighbourhood rather enjoyed it all, though the milkman, forbidden to clump in clogs down the street at Downham when sound tracks were being made, and the bus held up until shooting was completed, and cottagers kept waiting for their milk, thought it all "a bit much!" The film, *Whistle Down The Wind*, should do Lancashire a good turn, showing the world its pretty face.

Village architecture, Downham

When I bring my friends to Downham I watch their faces for reactions. Exiled Lancastrians dream about spots like this. We feel it is something to shout about. It is good to find a place which can have all modern amenities and improvements without being spoilt; electricity, telephone, piped water are here but without the usual obvious signs. This perfection did not just happen. It is the result of four centuries of constant vigilance on the part of one family.

When the Asshetons took over the hall of the Dinelays in 1558 it was centuries old then. Dunum means "many hills"; look around to count them. A perfect village plan, by stream edge and lane side, it clusters around a green, straggles up a hill, faces church and inn, and pulls up respectfully near the Hall gates. Take each detail of cottage and garden separately and it is satisfying; take the village as a whole—as Queen Mary did, framed in the church porch—or from the brand new village hall up the Brow, or from the bridge, or from the doddering sycamore which shadows the stocks by the bus terminus and post office—and it leaves nothing for criticism.

The architecture: Tudor building at Well Hall, Fir Tree Cottage near the bridge, seventeenth-century walls at Lower Hill below the churchyard; eighteenth-century handloom weavers' houses round the green, and the Hall in its own quiet gardens beyond the church, a sixteenth-century house enclosed within a classical but simple Georgian façade. The church; ancient tower and font, but a spacious and filled-with-light nave built a century ago.

Overheard in the village.

"Doctor told my husband years ago he'd not much longer to live. Well, we came and got a cottage in Downham. And from that day he bloomed like a new plant!"

A sunny day and Downham enjoying a fête in the Hall grounds. Two elderly women sitting back in the sun and looking around them. "Some folks," remarked one, "has their Heaven on earth!"

Heard outside Downham.

"My brother was in the village last Sunday. He says it isn't what it used to be. They've spoilt it."

Downham *is* just as it used to be, but people come on Sundays because they love it, in cars and coaches. That is the penalty of being pretty. Too many come to admire.

LANES NORTH OF DOWNHAM

Unlimited contrast of scenery, including rather bare and often forbidding Pendle foothill country about Cold Weather Hills and Weets Hill, and enchanting cloughs with primrose banks, ferny ledges and cascades behind which dippers nest, as at Twiston, Howgill and Middop, make this countryside an all year round delight. From Downham Post Office; carry forward into the delicious dell by Twiston millpond, pass the greystone farm at Lowergates and on to the county boundary. Here Ings End sits astride the beck, near the banks where men once worked the Mines Royal in Craven, the York and Lancaster Lead Mines. It was here in Tudor times a Pudsay of Bolton Hall extracted silver from the ore, coining from it very good false shillings. Beyond, the lane goes on through the gate at Wytha farm, unfenced to Middop, where the seventeenth-century hall is fronted by the most colourful garden beds, and up to the highway from Colne to Gisburn.

Anyone who enjoys "lost lanes" should walk that which is parallel to this highroad. It is Coal Pit Lane, the old way to Gisburn, now returned to Nature, rioting with campions and ragged robin, wild roses and honeysuckle, the runnels bright with marsh marigolds and blue with forget-me-nots in their season.

Stray on a wrong road and the odds are you find yourself at Martin Top chapel, or at Newby, or Stopper Lane, all outlying hamlets near Rimington. Or lanes deep within screening hollies, rowans, thorns and ashes, which coax spring flowers to show their heads in early March and induce summer flowers to bloom into October, send you hithering and thithering into Howgill or Gazegill. These byways, insinuating themselves into hidden corners of the county, are not overcrowded; which is just as well, they are so narrow.

From Downham Hall gates; here forks the Rimington road to Downham Mill Bridge, over the border and away. The country on either hand is green and pleasant; paths galore tempt us to wander. Two of my own favourite walks begin just above the bridge.

From a stone slab gap stile on the left the path drops across pastures to Swanside Beck and its much photographed humpbacked bridge. Less than ten minutes walk and you are by the stream.

Take a March day; pheasant fly on powerful wings into the larch wood, a pair of wild duck rise from a pool and circle overhead squawking. Curlews, newly arrived, wail around the valley, sweet and sad. Look for the whitest white patch by the stream; it is the dipper's bib, obvious as he bobs and flirts with his own reflection.

This path continues downstream to Smithies Bridge and the busy A59 near Sawley.

Back to the Rimington lane. A farm track opposite the stone stile heads for the old mill in an enchanting hollow by Ings Beck. Beyond the farmyard are green pastures and sunny silence.

Wood pigeons are crooning, thrush and blackbird going it, wrens and robins carolling away. A white-breasted treecreeper runs mouse-like up a tree and pirouettes in downward flights. A canary yellow bird flies by—and another; a pair of wagtails.

Around Downham Mill farm, by the overgrown millpond and the empty mill race is bird song incessant and chuckling water music.

At higher level, on the smooth limestone slopes of Downham Green and the Fairy Rock, March days have moments of good humour. A family of leverets, five of them, chase each other in mad circles till we are dizzy watching their movements. More handsome red-brown hares jump and stamp and set off in haywire gambollings all around the limestone knolls. And all the time sheep graze without lifting a head and curlews wail and circle over.

The Chase and Royal Forest of Pendle

I once heard a broadcast in which a reference was made to the "dark and gloomy forest glades" through which the Pendle witches scurried to their unholy Sabbaths. A wrong conception.

Lancashire has many regions named as Forests, but none has the remotest resemblance to Sherwood or Savernake or the New Forest, and never had. Pendle, Trawden, Rossendale, were among the estates of Edward the Confessor appropriated by the Conqueror in Blackburnshire and considered suitable for the royal pleasure of hunting.

The Norman conception of Forest was open country given up to the beasts of the chase for the king's pleasure solely. The rights of the natives mattered little. Forest laws were devised, and to see they were kept forest officers appointed, foresters, verderers, and courts held at regular intervals to deal with crimes against the "vert"—the herbage and trees, and "venison", the animals.

Forests were king's land but there were Chases too, portions of afforested country granted to lords in favour with the king, which came under common law. Pendle was a chase, granted to the de Lacys of Clitheroe Castle, part of the great Forest of Blackburnshire. The de Lacys also held the Hodder valley, the Chase of Bowland, lying over the Yorkshire border.

To reserve forest or chase wholly for game was not a paying proposition: therefore farming was encouraged in small pockets where the bleak and inarable soil would respond a little. In Pendle, small communities grew up around the first enclosures or "Heys"; the herdsmen built for themselves "Booths" and "Folds" to shelter the animals. These cattle-breeding and dairy farms, known as vaccaries, from the Norman French *vache*, were cared for within the chase and became eventually the townships of Goldshaw, Barley, Rough Lee, Wheatley and Old Laund.

Around them the deer still roamed the hills, had freedom to browse in the oats grown by the men of the booths—and none could chase them out or keep dogs to set on them—and were encouraged to leap fences, banks and ditches of Launds designed for their reception, there to fatten for venison. Old Laund and New, the launds of Fencegate and Hewn Achelor "where herds of stags had their living", and the Calder side deer park at Ightenhill were all valuable preserves.

Many of the interesting old farms we pass when walking along Pendle foot, each one in its own clough by its own stream, were built in the reign of Henry VII by tenants who had been encouraged to enclose forestland. A century later their security was shattered.

Forest farm, Lowerhouses

James I employed lawyers who discovered that Pendle copyholders could not pass their holdings from father to son. Imagine the shock to grandsons of these with Henry VII grants!

Said James, "You are only tenants by sufferance, your lands are assart." Assart lands were grants the new tenants were allowed to clear of trees, to farm and cultivate as long as crops would grow without using manure; when the land no longer gave increase—back to the forest, back to lord, duchy or Crown. Great families of Calderdale, yeoman farmers, and lesser folk, were all involved in James' ruling.

Only because he was short of ready money did the King come to terms, deciding to have their titles confirmed on payment of twenty years' rent, further relenting and accepting twelve years' rent. There the matter ended.

Pendle Forest, remote from the outside world, looking with suspicion on all incomers, cut itself off from outside influences. It held on to old customs, superstitions were rife. Nowhere was a better breeding ground for ideas which led to black magic, practice in diablerie, for witch cults. Neglected in the interim period following the end of Whalley Abbey, certain ignorant and simple folk joined in what they called Covens, met at Sabbaths where they indulged in strange rites, united in worship of the devil, and altogether found it a profitable business, for their neighbours were intimidated, terrorized and blackmailed very easily.

Pendle had not the monopoly of witches but seems to have attracted the most notice. Lancashire's witches were the ones playwrights in London wrote about. Poets too had something to say.

Old Mother Demdike and Company

Who were the Pendle Witches?

They were real people living in the Pendle villages in the reign of James I, a monarch who believed implicitly in the power of witchcraft. Enlightened travellers wrote of them as " poor old wives who in those desert misty moors do dwell, hungry and cold ", with no priest to give them " ghostly counsel ".

Richard James journeying through Lancashire in 1636, after a second witch trial, wrote of Malkin Tower, meeting place of Covens, as :

> " ——a little cottage, where
> Report makes caitiff witches meet to swear
> Their homage to the devil and contrive
> The deaths of men and beasts—— "

Foremost among the witches was Elizabeth Southernes who as a young married woman sold her soul to the devil and finally became " the devil's chief agent in these parts ". She was heartily feared as Old Mother Demdike, living in Malkin Tower, bringing up her children and her daughter's, Elizabeth Device's children, as practising witches. She also brought in Anne Whittle, later known as Old Chattox, into her master's service, a relationship which soon resulted in two families at loggerheads and bitter rivals, each quick to undermine the power of the other. Between them, the Demdike brood and the Chattox clan terrorized Pendle.

Others joined them—two Bulcock's of Moss End, the two Hargreaves of Thorneyholme, the two Howgates of Pendle (of Demdike stock), Old Mouldheels (Katherine Hewitt) and others, poor folk, easily suggestible. They doubtless took drugs—belladonna, aconite, opium—they probably believed they had done strange deeds, witnessed stranger ones, flown through the sky on broomsticks to hilltop sabbaths. If they insisted great powers were theirs, to maim or kill through witchcraft, then they could blackmail, demand what they wanted from anyone they chose, for everyone believed them.

Mistress Alice Nutter, widow of Richard Nutter of Rough Lee Hall, was of a different class, but suspicion fell on her too, and the Demdikes pulled her down with them so that at the trial in 1612 she too was condemned to death. Nineteen witches from Pendle and Samlesbury were tried, ten were found guilty, nine of them of the Pendle group. Old Demdike escaped the gallows by dying in her cell; she was over ninety.

The 1612 round-up of witches had been made on Good Friday at Malkin Tower. In 1633, the victims accused of witchcraft were said to have been at an unholy feast held at Hoarstones, not far from Higham. Seventeen were haled to Lancaster and condemned by the jury. But the Judge, not satisfied, instigated further enquiries, got the King interested and sent off a sample batch of witches to London to be examined and questioned by royal doctors. Also the boy, Edmund Robinson of Wheatley Lane, whose evidence had brought them to trial, was questioned. He broke down, confessing that his father and uncle had put him up to it, that his tales of what happened one dark night at Hoarstones were a pack of lies. They had prompted him when they did the rounds of country churches on Sunday mornings, to point an accusing finger at this woman and that, and if no money was paid into their hands to keep quiet, then they were said to have been seen at witches' sabbaths, partaking of unholy food, committing diabolical acts.

After 1633 no more Pendle Forest folk were tried for witchcraft, but tales were often told of queer goings-on.

I have heard tell of a farmer near Huntroyd who "hanged himself with his galluses because he felt he'd been witched", and of a field near Barley never, never, mown at haytime because witches long ago fouled a certain spot in it. I heard of two old ladies who came every year to place a wreath on the witch's grave—reputedly Alice Nutter's—in Newchurch graveyard; I talked to an old man who remembered the wife at Rough Lee Hall scribbling with a pottery mould all over the hearthstone, in large twists and twirls saying, "If I do this witches can't do any harm if they come down t' chimney; they'll get all tangled up."

Pendle folk used many charms in the old days. Red thread twined in a cow's tail when turned out to grass in May would prevent witches milking her. Horseshoes on a stable door would stop the horses being hag-ridden. Holed stones, found in a brook, were hung on hooks in the attic to keep evil influences out. A local historian in Clitheroe collected witch stones, an interest puzzling to a Pendle woman. Only one explanation came to her mind. "Is he that feared o' witches?" she asked. "Is he bothered wi' night mares?"

Trying to worm tales of witches out of Pendle folk is heavy going. They are quite in and of this world now and like everyone else take superstition lightly. All the old houses with their chimney "witch seats" are provided with T.V. aerials; what self-respecting witch would sit astride one of those?

Pendle Paths, East Side

One October day, climbing Clerk Hill above Whalley golf course, we saw mists playing strange tricks over the Calder, magnifying familiar heights, transfiguring the drab towns up the valley as sun's rays bursting through played searchlights over roofs and chimneys.

Many paths cover the hills near Whalley, a very pleasant one, our choice, becoming a grassy way between the conifers of Bab House Wood, crossing the ridge through Wiswell Moor quarries and slanting down open pastures to Sabden.

This village in the valley has its feet in two worlds. Once it was a great place for loading and reloading of packhorse trains; several villagers were eighteenth-century haulage contractors with stables full of packhorses. It became industralized in Victorian times with Richard Cobden's mills drawing attention from enlightened employers of labour; he had schools for the children, library and institute. It began to grow along old roads. It spread along the valley floor but retained Pendle and the high moors for its confines and a sky full of lark song, curlews crying and cuckoo calls for its ceiling.

One road forges upwards to the Nick of Pendle, another rushes down from Black Hill, both part of the ancient cross-country route known before Norman times. A farm track to Sabden Dean follows the brook into the Forest. A lane which begins behind the stream-edge cottages called Heyhouses and, turning by the Tudor house called Cockshutts, wriggles between hollies and thorns to Ratten Clough. This was our choice. It is bonny in October.

Ratten Clough, Cock Clough, Stainscomb, Churn Clough name the ravines and deep hollows in Pendle's eastern flanks. On the map look for the Devil's Apronful, where the Old Lad dropped the stones he intended to destroy the castle at Clitheroe, the Devil's Footprint in the rocks behind Craggs farm. These, and other fascinating names recalling wilder days, are thick upon the bronze-brown face of the hill.

Stainscomb fascinates me. It is a vast bowl within the arms of Pendle, clad in tawny bracken, threaded by little streams, these joining as they run down to a Tudor farmstead of the same name. It is now sad and empty; looking through the mullioned windows or through the holes in the pegged door within the porch we find animals peering out, maybe a black Aberdeen Angus bull or young calves. Out of the silence as we turn away we hear the faint mewing of a kestrel hovering high above.

Stainscomb's field walls are moss-encrusted flagstones, upended, but from Cock Clough farm to Sabden Fold and Newchurch, grass track, farm track and lanes alike are defined by hollies and thorns, always the same trees which, in Forest days, were shelter to animals and, the holly, winter feed when all else was under snow.

All the farms we passed were part of the old Forest scene. The one least changed and recognizable for what it was in Tudor days is Sabden Great Hall, a comely house with sloping gardens, huge sheltering beeches, a clear well at its gate and the sun smiling on its face. The road twists and turns round its walls, then is hurled round to the brant hillside.

How the lane climbs! Deep below banks and boulder-built walls it is one of the first to be blocked by winter's snowdrifts. Heather moors on one hand—and Ling Bob, once home of a besom maker who used ling as raw material of his trade—and a hollow, once marshy land, on the other. Many stiled footpaths join Meadow Top and Bull Hole, a walk which according to the trial evidence of the Pendle witches was one Chattoxes and Demdikes frequently took.

Countrylovers must not be surprised to find an occasional chimney of a factory intruding into the Pendle landscape. There is one at Spenbrook and another half hidden by Pendle Water at Narrowgates. In spite of these Pendle is quite capable of pulling down the curtains and shrouding itself in mystery. If you are susceptible it is possible at the witching hour of "dayleet gate" you will have "feelings too strange to relate". Which should "make your day".

Primed by your reading you will look for Malkin Tower. No one is sure where it stood, but possibly it was sited in one of the "malkin fields" near Newchurch. Malkin is name for a hare, but we hear of witches giving this as a term of endearment to their cats, their very familiar spirits. A hare speeding across these acres long ago might have been a witch, able to change her form at will!

There certainly were queer goings-on in these parts, no doubt about it.

Old Demdike, sightless old hag, shuffled this way tapping with her stick, clinging to the arm of Alison, her granddaughter, still muttering curses on forest folk who had dared to thwart her. Old Chattox too, "her chin wagging, her lips muttering men knew not what", often trudged the lanes to Newchurch leaving a trail of consternation behind her, her curses ringing in the ears of Nutters of Bullhole, of Moores of Dean.

Nearer our time were the Kirk Gang, a band of men who robbed lonely Pendle farms, stole hams and sides of bacon at night and found a table-top grave, near the church porch, a safe larder. Tales are told of them and heavy doors shown with marks of their attacks.

Newchurch, when it was Goldshaw Booth, kept close to the hill-side and every dwelling borrowed shelter from its neighbour, just as now where a street of high, narrow houses leaps to the hilltop without a break.

Many of the Pendle witches and wizards were regular attenders at the New-Church. The "eye of God", a symbol carved in stone on the tower was on them, for this is the original fabric. The Witch's Grave is at the door. And for the diversion of tired walkers, a gravestone to locate, carefully lettered but deficient in punctuation.

The last two lines of the epitaph—

> "Rest for the weary way,
> Sore feet rest from all labour now"!

Newchurch-in-Pendle

No one can leave Newchurch without climbing up or dropping down. To Barley it is up, and steeply down, by the road or, the way we took, up the stony alley called "up Bastille" and field path over to Ogden Clough and Barley Green.

Once hag-ridden, Barley is now a quiet spot; the only witch flies across the inn sign—harmlessly. A few rows of houses, knots of cottages sideways to the street, others huddled in sheltered alleys, one or two old farms with long adjoining shippons and barns, a chapel building—there is little else. The general impression is of a community close-packed for companionship and protection from the elements.

North of Barley the Downham road toils up towards Pendle and its formidable " Big End ", but on foot a path from Windy Harbour and over Turf Fields (no longer used for peat cutting) takes an easier route, the two meeting near Annel Cross, four lanes end.

East of Barley, following Pendle Water, the highroad to the world of industry and commerce takes one bank and a very pleasant way for walkers, the other. One goes up and down to Thorneyholme whilst the path links the quiet cottages in the Narrowgates mill yard with Whitehough, the proud house on site of a Keeper's Lodge in Forest days, built in 1593 " by Christofer Bullocke and Jenet his wife ", and green fields of the valley floor take pedestrians happily to the river at Rough Lee.

If you expect a rendezvous with witches, or the slightest touch of diablerie here you are bound for disappointment. Be prepared for shocks—Happy Valley and tea rooms, Lido and Palm Beach caravan and chalets, and contrasts. Old-fashioned villagers look out over the pot plants of cottage window-sills, called Ivy, Lilac, Rose.

Of course you want to locate Rough Lee Hall, home of Mistress Alice Nutter, a witch of the 1612 trials. What you expect to find will depend on what you have read and you will react accordingly. The Hall is at the far end of the village; it stands well back from the road with a narrow lane called Straight Gate running by its walls. Does it look at all odd?

It is a good example of the kind of halls Tudor families, the prosperous merchants or yeoman farmers or small landowners built for themselves. This gabled building with most interesting diagonal chimneys was built by the substantial local Nutters—the date seems to be 1536, though the carving is worn—whose son married a woman they obviously disliked. When he died suddenly, after hard drinking and hard riding, they accused the widow of having a hand in his death. When the suspicion of witchcraft fell on her they raised no finger to help.

Forest Byways

Seventeen miles of road encircle Pendle. To perambulate the Forest bounds is a matter of nineteen miles, every road being as crooked as a dog's hind leg.

One scenic route for motorists is as follows:

From Whalley by Portfield, Read Old Bridge, turn by Cob Carr Nook, follow hill ridge to Padiham Heights, Black Hill and Stump Hall, then down to Sabden Great Hall. The lane—take it with care—

Old guide post at Annel Cross

carries up and round to New-church and up and on to Barley. The road to Annel Cross is near to Pendle, over windy wastes, old turf fields. Turn right at the four lane ends and down to Black Moss, once home of the Bulcocks, suspected witches. When the wind whistles over, imagine eldritch laughter in its undertones; wonderful gathering ground for witches hereabouts.

Lanes turn off to Rough Lee, very narrow and deep within old walls. From the village climb Nanny Maud Brow from the cross roads at Thorneyholme, striking along the Forest Boundary above Spenbrook, behind Hoarstones, where the 1633 gang of witches held their Sabbaths, carrying on to Harper Inn, through Fence (of the Forest) Higham, where forest courts were long held in the Hall (now a modernized farm), down to Padiham and the Calder where the horse closes and stabling for the king's chargers used to be.

The best map for exploring the Pendle country is Sheet 95 of the one-inch Ordnance Survey.

OVERHEARD AROUND PENDLE

A passenger on a local bus was saying, " We had a grand run in my brother's car yesterday. Sixty miles we went, all around Colne and Gisburn and Hellifield—and we never lost sight of Pendle. And do you know—it never moved ! "

Burnley friends were showing a Londoner these parts. They made a circular tour round Pendle. Later, amused, he commented, " That hill, Pendle, everyone talks about it—him—as if he were one of the family."

Church Lane, Whalley

II Calder Country

THE CALDER RIVER, which started as the Water of the Sun god, pure enough to be used for baptism of seventh-century Christian converts, has become a sorry spectacle, its polluted waters as Man has mis-used them. Countrylovers avert their eyes from the river itself, but need not avoid the valley, for history, architecture and old houses are its strong points.

Among larger halls are Towneley in its Park and open to all, Holme-in-Cliviger, a most historic home backed by woods, Gawthorpe starting on a new life of usefulness as college and residential cultural centre, also open to the public, Huntroyd, ancestral home home of the Starkies, and Read Hall, a gracious Regency house on the site of the home of the Nowells.

The smaller halls make a long list. Among them are Hacking Hall near the confluence with the Ribble and Hodder, Martholme, now a farmhouse not far upriver from Cock Bridge, Portfield from which masonry was taken to build an inn at Whalley, but which still has a splendid old barn with its original aisles and nave and massive posts and beams. Dunkenhalgh of the Walmesleys, now an hotel—

and many an old homestead which holds on to memories of better days before industry darkened its walls and towns overspilled on to its green acres.

History at Whalley

Centre of a parish four hundred square miles in extent—that was Whalley in the Middle Ages, the ecclesiastical heart of half Lancashire.

However eager you are to stand and stare, do not indulge in the main street or disaster might follow. Better for sessions of silent thought are Church Lane and The Pool—a welcome pool of quiet it is between church and abbey—or take the short steep pull from the bridge to The Nab top and meditate over Whalley mapped out for you.

Churchyard cross, Whalley

I wonder when the folk of Wallei did in fact hear the good news of Jesus Christ? Some believe King Edwin, when baptized by Paulinus at York in 627, sent out priests to teach the folk of outlying parts of Northumbria and they arrived at this Calder-side village. Once men tried to prove St. Augustine was here thirty years earlier.

In the churchyard are three tall crosses. No other church has so many, and all, according to the most conservative estimate, about a thousand years old. If they have a link with either St. Augustine or Paulinus it has never been proved. Rather do they show Celtic influence in their carving. Possibly priests of the Celtic church reached the Calder valley on missionary journeys from Iona.

The tallest cross makes one think; its panels, in low relief, show the Dove, Christ haloed and with hands raised, but beneath is carved a hound with head turned. Was this the Dog of Berser which Norsemen used as symbol of eternity and when they became Christian they associated it with God the Father?

Consider the limits of the old parish of Whalley. If you know your Lancashire, names, even in their old form, will be familiar.

From the meeting of Calder with Ribble the boundary followed the river to Rymingdon Water, that is to Swanside Beck at Smithies Bridge. Ings Beck took the boundary to Twyssulton Broke, through Midhope, to a certain oak "known as the Croked-oke in Admergill".

The next names are not so clear. Poundescaghead, Bernetknarres and Wolvestone obviously worked east, for "the cross under Wycoluer" comes later and we know it as Watersheddles Cross. On the parish boundary went, south to Scart-Super-Crowehull, by the Wetherstones of Bulswyre, thereafter following Stipersden to East Calder. It crossed Cliviger into Rossendale "by Belerclough and Sharneyford"; following the Irwell "down the descent of water to Uggesden, and north to a hill called Uggelow"! Piked Lowe is named and then "by Knowesden and Hyndburn" back to the Calder.

In his will of 1296, Henry de Lacy granted the monks of Stanlaw the parish of Whalley. They arrived and for over two centuries, until 1534, the Abbot was to wield tremendous power over a wide area.

Where the Dean of Whalley had formerly been all powerful, now it was the Abbot. All roads ran to Mother Church, and from the Abbey roads set out to the many daughter churches served by monks as their priests. How busy they must have been with their loads of tithes, all forms of produce and trading, and behind the cavalcades of great lords seeking hospitality at the abbot's table, many humbler wayfarers making to the abbey's west gate for a night's shelter.

Though the parish church was nearly seven centuries old when the abbey took shape, it has within it many links with abbots and monks.

Near the font look for the elaborate stone grave lid of the last Dean, Peter de Cestria, at whose death the grant of his kinsman de Lacy came into effect. In the north chapel read the inscription on the screen telling that Thomas Lawe, Monk, was priest here, and nearby find the tomb lid thought to be that of John Paslew, last abbot, executed in 1537. In the chancel the canopied choir stalls, with a fine collection of carved miserere seats, are among the treasures of the church.

These monks' seats were made for the abbey choir and only brought here after the abbey was dismantled. Each is carved and there are some good fifteenth-century quips among them.

One was a comforting thought to the celibate; a home-returning warrior is being belaboured by an irate wife brandishing a ladle.

Another, unique among misericords, shows the shoeing of a goose, its legend being that "he who melles (meddles) must" could find no better occupation than this difficult task. On one the goose is being carried off by a fox to a den with peeping fox cubs, whilst the woman sleeps over her distaff. A coy maiden turns her cheek from a wooing satyr. The Emperor Alexander is carried into the sky by flying dragons, to survey his dominions.

A visit to this church is a complete history covering thirteen centuries. An excellent guide book explains all.

When the monks took up residence at Whalley they occupied the Rectory, which had been the Deanery, and used the chapel of de Cestria—which is the oldest part of the ruins as we see them today—until their new quarters were ready. Monastic buildings, starting with the west gate and its chapel in 1319, and ending with the building of Lady Chapel, Abbot's new lodgings and north-west gateway, lasted throughout two centuries. After which, dissolution brought quick un-building in its train.

Look for carved abbey stones in late sixteenth- and seventeenth-century farms, halls and churches not so far from Whalley. It is thought Old Langho church made use of abbey masonry for its outer walls in the 1550s and the Southworths acquired stonework for their family chapel and parlour windows at Samlesbury Hall.

The abbey is a silent backwater where one can dream away the sunny hours of a summer's afternoon—lulled by birdsong and bees droning, watching the play of light and shade on the aged stones, idly noting the lengthening shadows stealing over lawns and garden plots. The grass which carpets nave and transepts, choir and chancel, is soft underfoot. The high walls of cloister and dorter make the cloister garth a suntrap into which cold airs cannot enter. Along the Calder bank the long walk, an avenue arched over by tall trees— a choir for feathered choristers—slows down the exploratory progress of all visitors. Without knowing it they, one and all, assume the slow sacerdotal tread; even the boisterous have no desire to raise their voices. That is the effect the abbey has; is it some restraining influence still at large, left over after so many centuries,

"When Time ran smoothly from Matins to Evensong"?

The Nab and the Dean

Stand on Whalley bridge and watch traffic stream by. This was always the busiest Calder crossing, first a ford linking Wallei and the settlement of seventh-century Billingas, then as site chosen for the bridge, the stone for which Adam de Huddleston gave a quarry in the nearby moors, in the early fourteenth century. The time was when the Cistercians were getting into stride with their new abbey building plans and much activity was centred here.

From the south end of Whalley bridge; the old, pre-turnpike road drops down from The Nab in a series of sharp bends, under beeches, between high holly hedges. The terrace walk of a road onwards once took monks to Blackburn church, abbots riding forth on business of their House, and in June 1644 it echoed to galloping of Prince Rupert's cavaliers on their way to take Clitheroe Castle and relieve beleagured Skipton.

Narrow packways toil up The Nab to lose themselves in the deep gullies of the Dean; here is a secret nook of Lancashire—and oh, so near to towns!

Keep away from these Nab top lanes if you are in a hurry. These ways were designed for local farmers, not for reckless drivers, so go warily, or leave cars down in Whalley when on discovery bent.

Among the good things " up above " are the wide landscapes seen from the highest point—where Bel of the Billingas had his seat, Belsetenab. It is a fine survey of the best country dealt with in this book, all Pendle and the green places of the Forest are in it, the Calder from its watershed to meeting with the Ribble and Hodder, and the Ribble from high dale in Craven to gentler valley and the estuary. You may look for the fair gap where the Hodder breaks through from Bowland Forest and scan the sky over Longridge Fell for the weather to come. Rain clouds and good weather reach us by way of Chippingdale.

" We had more than one fine view in ascending Nabs Hill," wrote a traveller in 1840, " and found the prospects amply repaid the labour."

What local children call " Roman stones " are in fact discarded, half-finished upper and nether millstones, lying in the heather on the hilltop, where craftsmen left them a century or so ago. The workshop was among rocky outcrops, for us a fine viewpoint.

The sunny valley below is The Dean and the round-topped hill above it is the fairy knoll of Bowley, enchanting on a Spring day when lark song is loud over the lambing pastures.

Pleasant paths above The Dean link farms and ruins; they wander to the reservoir and the skyline above Whittle Hall and the hamlet called New York.

What an outspread landscape! Brace yourself against the wind and let your eye rake moors, fells and far-away mountains. Men and boys go striding by with whippets and greyhounds. Scots beef cattle look at you through towsled fringes. And sometimes children come to fly their kites.

These Billington Moors have an all-the-year-round attraction for
out-door lovers. A century ago they were notorious for gaming
schools where gangs of men played games like knick-knack and pitch-
and-toss, and cock fighting was not unknown; but now the walkers
we see are law-abiding countrylovers from nearby towns.

In winter, flocks of immigrant birds seek the reservoirs and the
upland pastures, among them large gatherings of plover, fieldfares
and especially starlings. The conifer plantations on The Cliffe provided roosts for numbers popularly estimated as "millions" during
the winter of 1959-1960. Their nightly manoeuvrings brought crowds

Fairy hill, Back o' Bowley

to see them and were a perpetual headache to the water engineers
and farmers alike. Countless seedling elder trees are the result of
their sojourn.

I remember seeing a Calder side field, silent in December, suddenly
fill with clamour from thousands of birds as they dropped in a dense
cloud from the sunset sky. Every tree became black with them. In
turn formations flew away, to Billington Moor and beyond, until
all had gone.

One evening walking The Nab road, Moor Lane, I was conscious
of a sound like heavy rainfall and looked up to see invasion of
successive formations of starlings, some flying low enough to weave

in and out of the treetops in the beechwood. Their wing beats were loud as a heavy shower. All converged upon the nightly roost.

Ancient Houses and Historic Sites

A Calder side footpath runs near the river from Whalley Bridge to Cock Bridge, near the Game Cock Inn. Walk uphill to Cop Hall where a lane goes off to Martholme. Turn over the bridge, take the lane by the nursery gardens, and you come to the lodge gates of Read Hall. Both are historic houses.

In the thirteenth century the Fyttons lived in a moated manor house on Mart-holme, by a Calder ford. An heiress married a Hesketh—the name also associated with Rufford—and one of that family, Sir Thomas, had major part in the hall as we know it. Returning safe and sound from campaigns in Scotland, he embarked on large rebuilding plans. He added the south wing, the very handsome gatehouse which carries on a carved shield his initials and date, and other work of his doing belongs to the period between 1561 and 1577. Robert, his son, also left his mark on Martholme in 1607. For centuries the Hall has been a farmhouse.

Read Hall of the Nowells had a very different fate. Known far outside the limits of Calderdale were two Tudor Nowells. Alexander was one who helped to write the Church of England Prayer Book, possibly The Catechism; he was Dean of St. Paul's, early head of Westminster School, the discoverer—by pure chance—of the merits of bottled ale, and received an admirable write-up in Walton's *Compleat Angler*, for a very keen fisherman he was. His brother, Lawrence, was Dean of Lichfield. A generation later (in 1612) Roger Nowell, that "religious honest gent", made a name for himself by his efforts to wipe out witchcraft in this area; the Pendle witches came to his home for interrogation and he was instrumental in their arrest.

An eighteenth-century Nowell, Alexander, spendthrift and squanderer of his family fortunes, brought about the ruin of his house. All was sold and the Hall passed into the hands of the Forts, who decided to pull down the Tudor house. They called in the Regency architect, Webster of Kendal, to work for them. Gillow of Lancaster designed much of the interior. They created a fair house. You catch a glimpse of its pillared portico and façade from the end of the drive. Within are lovely gardens and such an air of remoteness you can hardly believe that the towns of Calderdale lie outside its screening trees.

From outer Lodge to garden gate the drive is a public footpath; turn left along the track and field path and you are above Sabden

Brook. At Read Old Bridge history was enacted one April morning in the second year of the Civil War—in 1643.

The Queen had commanded Lord Strange—soon to become Earl of Derby—to bring the Lancashire Royalists across country to join her in Yorkshire. Ever loyal, he led his troops to Whalley, rested at the abbey overnight and when morning came sent ahead of the main force a scouting party. They never got beyond the old bridge behind Read Hall, for a small but indomitable party of local Roundheads waited in ambush in the narrow lane above Sabden Brook.

A burst of firing surprised the scouts as they came to the bridge. In turning they found their way blocked by the main force behind them. It was hopeless confusion—a rout—a catastrophe for the King's cause in the North.

Until 1961 a historic house surveyed the scene of the fight—the farm called Easterley—over the gate of which an escaping cavalier leapt, and away to inform the leaders of the Royalist forces of the tragic reversals. He was young Edward Tyldesley of Myerscough.

Above the bridge the lane toils up to Cob Carr Nook; the lane left becomes a delightful ridge road with the pleasantest prospects over the " Sape-deane ", to give it its first name. Hidden by the green wave of pastureland on the right hand is a long grass-grown " trough " which many thought was a prehistoric hollow way. The O.S. maps once marked it as Ancient Road or Roman Road, but the latest editions omit it. Most probably it was an old quarry " drift way " and local tales of hunted Royalists hiding in the dip, and witches scurrying along to be questioned by Master Nowell, mere inventions.

I am fond of this long lane, especially at dusk. Then—" Lo, the valley hollow, lamp-bestarred." A score of towns and villages springing into light, multitudes of lights, each cluster telling of some community, each dense mass of a town, each necklace, girdle, string of red, orange, amber, defining some Calder valley highroad.

Descend on one hand into the quiet vale where Sabden lies, and Pendle and the moors are a dark wall above; on the other into the villages on the fringe of The Forest, or into Padiham.

At the farther edge of Padiham is a most historic Hall which is destined in its great age to play a very active and lively role.

GAWTHORPE HALL AND THE SHUTTLEWORTHS

In 1599 the ancestors of Lord Shuttleworth began work at Gawthorpe, raising a fine late-Tudor dwelling around the heavy walls of a Peel which had already for many centuries watched a Calder ford. A few years ago it was offered to the nation as an ideal home for a residential cultural centre for men and women, from near and far. Before the offer was accepted an endowment of £50,000 had to be raised. Manchester University and the Lancashire Education Committee offered to provide lecturers and tutors for courses " in the arts and crafts of mankind ". Every public body on both sides of the Pennines has shown interest.

" Cherish the past; adorn the present; create for the future." With aims like this the Gawthorpe scheme ought to have everyone's support and go on from strength to strength.

A visit to Gawthorpe is not just another great house to be crossed off from the list of those " Open to the Public ". It is a memorable experience, doubly so for those fortunate to have had for guide the Hon. Rachel Kay-Shuttleworth, whose heart and soul is in this, the home of her ancestors. Not only do you see the Hall and its treasures of three and a half centuries, but her own treasures gathered from the four corners of the earth—a rare and priceless collection of embroideries, laces, shawls, tapestries, costumes, ceramics, textiles. They are to be kept here for the pleasure of all who wish to study what can be created " when heart, hand and eye work together ".

The approach to Gawthorpe is along a drive, through a thick avenue where the trees mercifully screen what the N.C.B. has done to the landscape. At the end, from the shade you merge into a pool of sunshine within which the ancient house glimmers with a dream-like effect, quite out of this world. The imagination is quickened. What a setting for high romance, you feel, looking up at the many transomed windows and bays, to the heart of the house, the high midmost battlemented tower.

I love old houses, but much more those whose account books are so detailed that I can find out who raised the walls, wrought upon stone and wood, where the material came from, how much the labourers were paid, and the names of those who came to the door and were welcomed as friends, or given money for their trouble, or sent away with alms and gifts.

It is good reading, this Gawthorpe Account Book. The first entry is in 1599 under " Mr. Laurence Shuttleworth touching his house ". From early entries we learn that some stone was quarried at hand, the freestone from Rycliffe on Padiham Moor. Neighbours sold timber trees, Mr. Bradyll from his wood near Whalley, Mr. Nowell of Read—great ashes, and Mr. Shireburne—large trees from Mitton Wood.

The workmen? Roger Cockshutt " fee-ed " the ground, that is levelled the site; John Baxenden set the foundations. Rearing day, June 1602, was a great occasion with a piper doing the honours. Every item is listed as the house rose from the ground; payment to masons who hewed the " window stuffe ", to the wright who worked on the "Starres in the middest of the Hall", to the man who made the "Hall dower in 4 days" and the Burnley smith who wrought the great lock for it. The Billington smith made the casement frames —44 days work. Gangs of masons, joiners, filled the place with their activities; then moved in the plasterers and their labourers—and up came the Whalley tanner "with fower score stone of haire to make plaister with".

The Great Hall with its fine minstrel gallery and huge chimney, up which small Shuttleworth children of the past sitting at their mother's knees "could see stars in the middle of the day", the magnificent fireplace and elaborate plaster ceiling of the parlour and equally splendid ceiling of the Long Gallery—all have a much greater appeal knowing who created such beauty.

The day came when the Hall was complete. Families dwelt happily in it, and in the kitchen quarters large numbers of household retainers and servants lived their own busy lives.

To the front door came at Yuletide the players of My Lord Dudley's, My Lord Derby's, Lord Monteagle's Companies, and the players and waits from Wakefield, Carlisle, Manchester. Little Shuttleworths danced excitedly to the music of pipers and fiddlers or watched with wide eyes the antics of the dancing bear. Constant visitors with famous and noble names were welcomed at the front entrance—and messengers from the homes of Shuttleworths married and living in scattered places—and messengers from London and Shuttleworths in Parliament, and bearers of urgent news in time of war.

But to the back door! Whatmough's boy, cow boy, brought his worn-out shoes for repair, and the shoemaker returned a surprising quantity of footgear repaired for the young Shuttleworths of the period 1612 to 1620. Never were children so hard on their shoes! The crow boy came for his pay "for keeping crowes furth out of the wheat" and the local midwife for her reward of 2s. 6d. for "helping a cow that could not calve". The maids welcomed James Shuttleworth "dish thrower" and up came, hot from their labours, "three wives and a maid who clipt the sheep". One arrived with new hoods for sparrowhawks and goshawks; another returned from a long journey to Warwick with a supply of Bamburie Cakes.

All the landowning families with hunting rights in Lancashire parks sent their keepers with frequent gifts of venison, whilst a stream of humble folk trooped up to Gawthorpe with small offerings —a little wench with winberries from Burnley Wood, Little Bill with a posy, Whipp boy with posies for mistress, Marie Ainsworth with strawberries, Horrabin from Whalley with apples and plums.

What distinguished visitors have been welcomed at the same Hall door! We learn so much of Gawthorpe, but how much more we want to know. Was Charlotte Brontë regretful when she and her husband refused the offer of Sir James and Lady Kay-Shuttleworth —the living of their new church at Habergham Eaves? They could not leave old Mr. Brontë, they said. A few months later Charlotte was dead.

TOWNELEY HALL

Another great and historic hall is sited by another Calder ford, beyond Burnley. Gawthorpe at present is open to the public only a few days during each of the Spring to Autumn months or by special application, but Towneley Hall is every day, from 10 a.m. till dusk, Sundays 2 p.m., and like other fine houses owned by corporations—free for all.

At Towneley was an early hunting lodge later enlarged into a Tudor mansion and altered to suit Georgian taste. Such contrasts it holds—dungeons of deepest dye, airy battlements—classical décor in the entrance hall as background for Charles Towneley's priceless collections of marbles from Greece and Rome (now in the British Museum). Down below, almost feudal kitchens where, amid the gear of preparing, cooking and dishing-up gargantuan meals, it is easy to picture from the past successions of greasy Joans and perspiring serving maids at work.

Poignant memories of the bad days of religious persecution linger in the family chapel with its fine Tudor panelling, old Sir John's praying stool and chair. Once it enshrined the skull of that loyal Jacobite Sir Francis; he was executed in London, and his head exhibited on a pike on London Bridge, until a faithful servant rescued it. Concealed between the floors of the house are hiding places, and in the attics Towneley supporters, sworn to aid the Jacobite cause, waited until time was ripe for them to sally forth.

In the Long Gallery doors open to reveal a number of rooms, each furnished to show a complete period of English furniture, a very rewarding study for those countrygoers who enjoy visiting country houses and know less than they would like to about period furniture.

One of the galleries contains a large glass case protecting several priceless works of embroidery, the silks bright and lustrous as the day in which delicate fingers worked the flowers, tendrils and leaves with them. It is thought these sixteenth-century vestments belonged to the Abbot of Whalley and were given to the Towneleys for safe keeping when Dissolution seemed imminent.

The road continues from Towneley into Cliviger, but to reach the upland hamlets and villages to the north take the Mereclough road and branch away to Hurstwood or Worsthorne.

Paths over the Deer Park of Towneley make for Red Lees from where walkers have a pathway approach to the Brun bridge near Omerod House (now " site of ") and up a steep pasture to Hurstwood at the edge of vast moorlands.

How quickly one escapes from the busy valley, the deep defile, the Gorge of Cliviger, which takes so much traffic through the Pennines and across the water shed of the two Calders! Below—the highroad the railway, the Calder-side communities large and small; above—a bleak moorland world, hardbitten, windswept, brown upland seamed by dark stone walls, intakes grazed by unkempt sheep with shaggy fleeces. The local Lonk sheep are common hereabouts and many breeders come to Cliviger Autumn Lonk sales. Revealed by the map are sites of camps, circles and burial mounds of prehistoric hillmen.

It is not to everyone's liking, this wild, almost Brontë-esque landscape, but I love it. It has an atmosphere all its own which " grows on you ".

Especially exciting are the walled-in tracks leaping from rocky cloughs to skyline ridges, and roads you can travel seeing only a rare motorist. Exhilarating and switchback ways follow the line of ancient routes, possibly used by travellers of prehistory and certainly by the Earls of Lancaster and the servants of the northern abbeys. The Long Causeway and the road by Widdop Gate into Trawden, both are of unknown age.

WORSTHORNE, HURSTWOOD AND WYCOLLER

Like beads on a string, or knots in old rope, a number of hamlets and villages are lined up along the bare moors above the upper Calder.

There is Worsthorne, with old-fashioned shops, low-browed cottages, a sprinkling of seventeenth-century houses, and old-fashioned folk to match standing about in The Square. Old-fashioned but hardly " pixilated ". But " pixilated " it was, just like Hurstwood, which can in some moods look more " fey ".

Both have prehistory at their backdoors. Both share the same tales of fairies, fairy women milking cows in the fields, churning and leaving gifts of tiny butter pats by nearby wells. They also blamed the fairies when odd, unbiddable children grew up in their midst, having a deep-rotted belief in changelings. Both were bothered by the same boggarts.

If you like old ways, then take Swain lane and a flagged path over open pastures to Hurstwood, not a mile away. It wears a remote air, as if it cared nothing for the busy world down in the valley. The brawling stream in the glen below is the same River Brun which gave Burnley its name. How differently age has treated them!

The first house, "builded by Barnard Towneley" in 1579, looks rather seedy and sorry for itself; it has come down in the world. Next is a pretty cottage, with a path disappearing behind its garden and losing itself in the hollow below. Facing is the most photographed house in Calderdale, rather self-conscious, knowing that in spite

Spenser's Cottage, Hurstwood

of its retiring position in a backwater people will search for it, and never dream of leaving Hurstwood without finding it. Just beyond, is Tattersall's Tenement, a farm without any pretensions to "prettiness", but which can hold its own in matters of age and history.

The first house by the bridge was once Hurstwood's proud Hall. The much photographed cottage is known as "Spenser's", for the poet, Edmund, was thought to be a visitor here during his college days, guest in an uncle's home. The farm was for generations asso-

ciated with the Tattersalls, a son of the family leaving home to
become servant to a duke. He was the Richard Tattersall who established the stables in Knightsbridge named after him, numbered the
Prince of Wales among his associates and guests at Highflyer Hall,
and among his patrons the Lord Bolingbroke from whom he bought
Highflyer, the horse, for £2,500. This was a good step from the day
when he bought "for a song" a besom maker's nag, a down-and-out
thoroughbred, put it out to grass, and later sold it for a handsome
profit.

A score of deep cloughs cut into the moors above the Calder, each
one bringing along merry streams from desolate places, past outlying
farms, by houses important in their time, then down to the outskirts
of Colne, Nelson, Burnley.

The pattern repeats itself. In every case the higher reaches are
made for the countrylover, full of surprises. I know green dells by
Thursden Water enchanting in June when bushes are pink with wild
roses and entangled with honeysuckle, and hilltops above Swinden
Water where, to lie on the soft turf and watch the white clouds
pile up in sun-shot palaces, is for many very heaven. Yet only a
mile or so away is hard-bitten country akin to the wuthering heights
just over the border.

They have character, all the moor-edge communities like Bottin,
Roggeram and Haggate—with names like that could they help it?—
and fine seventeenth-century halls like Extwistle, though too few
are left standing.

Where you least expect to find them, you come upon places which
have succeeded in holding on to the past against tremendous odds.

I am thinking of secluded hamlets like Wycoller about which most
Lancastrians have heard. It was setting for a novel *Mistress Barbara
Cunliffe*. Charlotte Brontë knew the place and many believe she
was thinking of the Hall when writing of Ferndean in *Jane Eyre*.

It could be a sad place "garrulous of better days", for—apart
from the few cottages and farms down in the Dean—there are many
overgrown and lost crofts, weed-covered waste ground once sites of
houses—and the Hall has long been roofless, ruinous. Yet summer
days at Wycoller are jolly days, happy families picnicking on the
greensward, children paddling in the stream and numerous active
youngsters fascinated by the many bridges clambering under and
over them. The Hall too is happy hunting ground for the adventuresome.

Hilarious lanes come leaping down from Trawden; pleasant paths
wander in from Laneshaw Bridge or Emmott Hall. And anyone who
is tempted upstream along the shadowy lane beyond the Hall finds
himself in an upland world of bright waters, flower-embroidered

meadows sloping down from skyline to water side, and high-perched farms at the edge of almost Alpine pastures. Boulsworth Hill is above and beyond; a lonely "outback".

You can *talk* about the past at Wycoller in the summer. In the depth of winter you can *feel* it. Then is the time when spectre horsemen come galloping through the night, ghosts of hunting squires following ghostly hounds over the aged one-slab bridge. Then you can imagine the roistering Cunliffes and their cronies drinking, gambling in their Hall—so empty now with the wind blowing eddies of brown leaves over the flagstones. It is not so easy on sunny days to picture the horror of Mistress Cunliffe when the hunted fox which sought her chamber for shelter was hounded to death before her very eyes; nor to credit the tale that a dying Cunliffe passed his last hours shouting encouragement as fighting cocks tore each other to pieces.

If you enjoy a hint of macabre, Winter is best for Wycoller.

THREE

BOWLAND, HODDER AND WYRE

Langden Bridge and Mellor Knoll, the Hodder Valley

I Hodder and Bowland

Hodder—Peaceful Water

THE CELTS NAMED the river well when they called it "peaceful water". It still merits the name for peaceful and pleasant it is, until spates send peat-brown floods down from Croasdale, Whitendale and Brennand to swell it.

Hodder is a shared river, used as boundary by twelfth-century "perambulators" to define Lancashire from Yorkshire. It takes a clever geographer to know in which county he is, for the border reels around without any apparent plan, leaving river and syke, to stride along high watersheds.

The Hodder is not coy: you can follow her by paths from bridge to bridge or by road along miles of her course. Lingerers on bridges watch the sun dazzle upon her ripples and rings made by trout on her deep pools; they watch the sand martins and sandpipers at Burholme, the heron at Thornyholme, the oyster catcher, the red-shank by Langden Holm and the bobbing dipper by the brink at Higher Hodder.

The walker knows her best in the intimacy of the Winckley Hall pastures, in the lovely Hodder Woods where progress is a scramble well worth while, and along her margin, bending under trailing branches between Sandal Holm and Doeford bridge. There is an enchanting stretch away from roads at Stakes stepping stones, and paths over limestone heights overlooking her within Little Bowland. From Burholme to Thorneyholme and Dunsop Bridge is "beauty born of murmuring sound", all a lover of river scenery can desire. The same delight goes all the way updale—when the pathfinder "sticks to his guns".

Walkers and motorists alike use the same fell road to track down the source of the Bowland watershed of Lamb Hill Fell. Though Lancashire does not cradle the infant river she is only a few yards over the border, so near that when the wind changes direction the raindrops destined for the Hodder blow over the skyline and augment the runnels and sykes of the upper Hindburn, a very lovely Lancashire river.

This fell country at the fountain head is very different from the meadow-footing course of the Hodder down by Whitewell and Chaigeley, and very remote from the woodlands of Mitton and Winckley.

The Chase and Royal Forest of Bowland

Where do Lancashire countrygoers stand when they wander in Bowland? Are they trespassing? Is this only "Lancastrian" by affection?

Yes, we must give Yorkshire its rights. One hundred and fifty square miles are firmly fixed within the West Riding. Only seven square miles were cut from the Forest in the twelfth century and, as Little Bowland, have always been "red rose" country.

Bowland has nothing to do with bows and arrows at all, though the foresters were doubtless good with both, but especially with the bill as a weapon. It is "bu" land, cattle country. Call it Bolland, like the natives do.

The Forest, like that of Pendle, derives its name from "foris", land devoted to the royal sport of hunting. Anglo-Saxon kings hunted this region and the Normans seized upon it too, taking in areas like Amounderness—the Fylde—which had been so devastated by rebellion in 1065 that it was good for nothing except afforestation.

Because the Conqueror gave Bowland, formerly Northumbrian territory, to his kinsman, Roger of Poictou, it was a Chase and so remained until his successors died out in male line; the de Lacy heiress married Thomas, Earl of Lancaster, her estates became his and on his execution after rebellion against Edward II they passed to the Crown.

The young king, Edward III, granted Bowland to his mother, Queen Isabella; she found organization of such vast and remote lands beyond her control so she disposed of Bowland and Blackburnshire in exchange for an annuity from chancery revenues—in 1348.

After this the King gave the estates to Henry of Lancaster. The Duchy was later created and Bowland Chase, being in royal hands, became the Forest of Bowland, a Yorkshire domain but a part of the Lancashire dukedom.

Soon, the kings of England realized more revenue came from farming by tenants—dairy farming and cattle ranching—than hunting preserves, so much of Bowland was turned over to other uses. There were already many "vaccaries"; after disafforestation others were added to them as more and more land was enclosed.

The new names on the Bowland map are recognizable after six centuries.

Pastures were taken in at Staple Oak (sometimes called Stump Oak), at Stotclose near Langden Holme, at Byrholm (Burholme), at Red Sike, which is the county boundary stream, as well as on the fellside at Bathacar, which might well be Beatrix or Baytricks.

There was a close at Harden, a swine pasture at Grisehurst, and Brocklehurst was fenced in. In Croasdale was a Lodge for William, keeper of the animals, who kept an eye on many enclosed cow pastures and horse closes, the animals having free range of the fells in the summer. The abbot of Kirkstall had leave to pasture his cattle in the new enclosures; already his horses were grazing on Brunghill Moor, at Battersby, Croasdale, Flatclough and at Woodhouse. There was "a little garden for pot herbs" at Hare Clough, and a sheep fold near The Lodge, which was probably site of the House of Croasdale.

Sheep were rare in forest areas; they could ill defend themselves from wolves.

For two hundred years many tenants took advantage of the waste-land enclosures, farming them, building houses for their families.

Slaidburn and Newton were growing "vills" encircled by the metes or boundaries of the forest. They were outside the actual chase but the villagers had to watch their step with regard to poaching, felling trees, fishing the river, owning dogs capable of chasing the deer, trespassing within the land under forest rule to cut rushes for thatch (a woman caught had her sickle taken).

Even when much of Bowland was farmed by leaseholders and many new prosperous yeoman farmers were getting well established, the area of hunting ground diminishing, the numbers of red deer and fallow deer decreasing, the forest laws still held. Families like the Tempests, Hoghtons, Stanleys, still considered the perquisites of being Master Forester worth having, and the forest courts continued to deal with offences against "venison and vert".

The manor house at Whitewell was also the Keeper's Lodge and Woodmote Courts held there dealt with offences against venison—that is against the beasts of the chase. Woe betide you if you were caught at Stable Stand, at Dog Draw, Back Bear or Bloody Hand—if the president of jury were not "on your side". The keepers were jury and the Master Forester, or his deputy the Bow Bearer, was president.

Halmote Courts, the courts of common law, were held at Waddington, and at Slaidburn, where the courtroom at the inn has been used within living memory; they dealt with offences against "vert", that is against trees, timber, brushwood, underwood, with trespass, escape of beasts of the plough into demenses, enclosures or woods, and with offenders who were seen carrying bows and arrows in the forest when off the king's highway.

The Bowland boundaries:

They must have been under constant review for perambulations were frequent. To give the limits simply—the Forest took in all the Hodder country and that of all its tributaries, from Hodder Foot to the skylines of Langden and Hareden Waters, the Trough Stone, Brennand and Whitendale, Croasdale and the Hodder Springs, runing east "as Heaven the water deals" from Lamb Hill to Bowland Knotts, and south, along the fell tops of Harrop, Grindleton, Waddington and Browsholme.

Neighbours of the Duchy were the Harringtons with their Chase, and the Percies and Mowbrays with their Fees.

By-roads through Bowland

HODDER UPDALE

Leave Whalley by the Mitton-Whitewell road, passing the Red Pump at Bashall Eaves, making the first place of call—a treasure house open to the public—Browsholme Hall.

At Browsholme Hall; home of the Parkers "time out of mind". The family were "park keepers" or "parkers" of the deer park at Radholme in the Middle Ages. For two centuries they cared for the limestone acres of Radholme Laund, but after rent-raising trouble with the first Tudor king Edmund Parker built a new home at Nether Brooksholme. Part of this Tudor hall was incorporated into the finer house erected of rosy-hued stone by a Parker who was Bowbearer of Bowland, Deputy to the Master Forester, in 1607—the Browsholme Hall we know today.

Generations of the family each added something to adorn or enrich their home, calling in fine craftsmen, architects and artists to do so.

Artists arrived, to paint portraits of brides in all their young loveliness, and sons full of manly pride about to set out on the Grand Tour. Here are portraits of court beauties of Lely's time, and for contrast the Old Keeper, a picture full of character, painted by Northcote out of his affection for the sitter.

What a list of great names are represented at Browsholme; the ornate work of Grinling Gibbons, Sheraton's handiwork and Chippendale's, the designs of Wyatt, Carr of York, Sir Charles Barry. And memories of the young artist, Turner, wandering around the country during a stay here, working on his drawings for Dr. Whittaker's *History*.

The highway on which Browsholme was situated brought many guests, welcome and unwelcome. There was always shelter here for certain kinsman who were Roman Catholic priests; the Hall had no secret hides as the isolation of the place was deemed enough security. In the Civil War years the house was unfortunate in being visited time and time again by commandeering and looting Cromwellian troops, who took all the horses, emptied the larders and demanded billets at the most inconvenient hours. In 1643 Colonel Briggs and his men carried off, besides a mixed bag of loot, " a grey mare—and one little boy taken prisoner to Thornton ".

The Parkers were known for their Royalist sympathies. One young Parker was " sent down " from Cambridge for daring to drink the king's health in public and eating a " lobster ", this being a byname for a Roundhead. All the valuables at Browsholme, all the silver vessels, were freely given to the king for melting down. One of the family was killed fighting for Charles; his riding coat is in the entrance hall, of soft doeskin, possibly hide of a Bowland deer.

The Parker who endured so much at Roundhead hands was promised compensation for his losses at the Restoration, but he had to wait so long before it materialized that he must have resigned himself to seeing nothing of it. Years later it came in useful to pay for the panelling of one of the handsomest rooms in the house.

The Hall is full of interesting things. One is a piece of needlework dated 1450, from the Radholme days.

" God bless Edmund Parker and all that wyth hym wonnes,
Hys wyf, five daughters and hys seven sonnes."

Another curiosity is the dog gauge, a Forest relic. When tenants grew crops they were allowed to keep small dogs, but none "bigger than will go through a stirrup", for the purpose of chasing the deer away. The size was determined by a gauge at Browsholme. If too big, and therefore a danger to the king's deer, it had to be expedited or a foot mutilated to slow it down.

Although obsolete, this inhuman law was carried out as late as 1780. John Parker was candidate for parliament that year, his opponents the Towneleys who, to queer his pitch, accused him of law breaking. His beagles would not pass the test, they said. Therefore the pack was destroyed.

Another odd relic at Browsholme is the skull of a relative martyred in the penal times. It rested quietly in a chest until a young Parker, home from Harrow, decided to play a prank which had unforeseen consequences. The skull disappeared. There followed many mishaps; ceilings caved in, beams collapsed. Re-building had to be done. Not until young Thomas retrieved the skull he had buried in the garden did things return to normal.

TO WHITEWELL AND BURHOLME

Leaving the Hall the road passes under fine chestnut trees on its way to Cow Ark, where the old Hall Hill road climbs up and over to Whitewell, passing the green, green pastures of Radholme Laund, deer park, vaccary—a precious piece of land enclosed within the royal forest. How fair the scene outspread, "calling home the heart to quietness" on April evenings, on blue summer days!

From Hall Hill top with the green serenity of the Radholme pastures about one, and a heart-rending lovely Bowland scene ahead, we feel as though Time has stood still. The landscape of the Hodder valley and the green hillocks of Little Bowland beneath the sombre Bowland fells must have looked little different in forest days.

There is an engraving in Dr. Whittaker's *Craven* showing the Whitewell scene about 1800, with the church and inn by the river, a farmer crossing the stepping stones to Laund House, men driving laden packhorses along the road, deer feeding in New Laund fields —and quite recognizable to us. A new stretch of road, small trees grown tall, a wayside inn less humble—little changed.

Three centuries earlier, travellers bound for the perilous Trough road stopped at a tiny chapel where the church stands, called for refreshment at a wayside inn where the hotel is, and hobnobbed with the "keeper of the fallow deer", who, as a Forest official, was allowed Whitewell Lodge for his use and a plot of ground near by "encompassed by a hedge" for his two horses. Many paused to watch seasonal activity around the Courthouse where Woodmote courts were held, to which all Forest tenants had to come to give account of their doings.

Burholme has changed a great deal. There is an ice-cream stand at the bridge end and people parking by the river. A fair bit of country; the bridge throws two graceful eighteenth-century arches over the Hodder, with a tempting field path going off on one side and a grey road leaping towards Little Bowland on the other.

The path leads to Burholme farm. You would never guess that centuries ago it was a sizeable hamlet with many dwellings where there are only rough ridges on the ground, and a forest chapel where now are only faint foundations, a carved corbel stone, red incised tiles, and a stone discovered which might have been its altar.

"They say Abbot Paslew once slept here," remarks Mr. Hazel-wood the farmer. Was it on a fateful journey to Lancaster for trial?

The farmer is one of Her Majesty's oldest tenants and proud of meeting his landlord at a royal garden party. The Duke made straight to him and asked him, and the other Duchy tenants, why they were so far from home on such a fine hay day.

"Haymaking can wait a day or two," Mr. H. replied, "but this chance to meet Her Majesty won't."

A pity the Queen cannot see her tenant farmers on their own ground; no acres in her Duchy are lovelier.

North of Burholme Bridge the road soon passes Hodder Bank, where the "Stot Close" was, comes to Langden Holm—where the brook is "more stones than watter"—and the Trout Hatchery from which so many rivers are stocked.

One farm nearer the Hodder is Root, which made a name in sporting circles when, a century ago, the Derby winner, Kettledrum, which belonged to the Towneleys, was at stud here. He sired Lady Langden, among whose progeny was the famous Persimmon.

A signpost says To Lancaster via The Trough. Tempting, but as we are following the Hodder to its source that road must wait and we turn by the eighteenth-century guide-post into Dunsop Bridge.

FROM DUNSOP TO SLAIDBURN

Dunsop has always held a watching brief along the many dales, but has done little about it apart from catering, formerly, for horse travellers at a smithy, and now for motorists at its garage. There is always the sound of flowing water about it and promise of good things ahead.

The Hodder now waters a dale of impelling loveliness. The floor of it is a series of parklands with fine timber trees, each surrounding an old hall or a large mansion. Flocks and herds feed in the greenest of pastures each defined by white limestone walls. On both sides the landscape has a cared-for-down-the-centuries look—as well it might.

What pleases me is the absence of poles, wires and cables. Electricity and telephone communications are here—but underground or so carefully sited that few poles are visible.

Like all the best byways the lane to Newton has its tales of macabre. Near the place where Rough Sike runs from the pastures by the Sugar Loaf into the fields of Knoll Haw, was once a Gallows Hill—therefore strange sounds reported at dead of night, "rattling of gibbet irons, groans, and a strange something not to be described", but enough to send terrified wayfarers scurrying onwards.

What a comfortable welcoming look Newton wears; an honest to goodness place with cosy memories of homespun and spinning wheels. In local annals it has rarely hit the headlines though it sat astride a forest highway—from Wigglesworth to Dunsop and Lancaster—had a Roman ford below its bridge and kept an eye on all who came and went "o'er t' fell".

It has no church, but a follower of George Fox penetrated into Bowland and so impressed Newtonians that a Meeting House for Friends was founded here; you can find it up a bylane, the date 1767 over its door and a tiny Sepulchre nearby, sighed over by whispering trees. In 1757 John Brabbin left twenty guineas to start a school for Quaker children and "poor children not being Quakers". This was a centre for education fifty years later when a timid boy called John Bright was sent to receive instruction under the Irishman, Francis Wills.

Thirty boarders and six village lads enjoyed school—rare in those days. They learnt to swim in the Hodder, to fish, explored local lead mines and caves, had trips to Clitheroe and mixed play with work nicely apportioned. The school was in a house near the first village store, on the left entering from Dunsop: look for date on wall.

Like every road entering Slaidburn, the one from Newton tumbles into the village, after passing the back of Dunnow and the tree-shadowed brow at Blue Butts. How beautifully the church and houses are framed for our delight, lying in a pool of sunlight in an emerald setting!

The sun rests on the giant steps of the pastures on the left hand —they are probably ancient strip lynchets—and on the river meadows to the right, where long ago my father and his friends camped in spite of the efforts of local lads to scare them away, fearing the smart youths from Clitheroe would steal away the village maidens' affection. This could not happen today; every eleven-plus Slaidburner leaves the village to acquire further education in Skipton, Clitheroe or in Ribblesdale and no longer suspects the ulterior motives of "outsiders".

No place looks more inviting than Slaidburn from any one of its four road approaches. It improves on closer acquaintance. The church with its tall thirteenth-century tower and fifteenth-century "body" has even older relics to show; an "angel stone" very like Norse carvings in Manxland, thought to be tenth-century work, and a cylindrical font from Norman times which an "improving" hand has smoothed are both from an earlier edifice.

Slaidburn village

The church beckons on the approach from the south so let it be the first place of call.

Familiar local names appear again and again on the tombs, on the eighteenth-century table tops and humbler, lowlier headstones, but of men who lived when the church as we see it was new—the Smiths, Quelwrights and Milners, Woodwards, Haywards and Cowherds—no record, nor of the villagers who bore provocative names like Paytfin, Halepenny, Jaknave and Playnamour! There was a Floyter too—the villager piper?

In many ways this is an unusual church. Slaidburn either kept to early forms of worship or went its own sweet way oblivious of the world outside Bowland. The communion table—no altar—the preaching, with the rector wearing Geneva black gown and "tabs", the saying instead of singing of the psalms, all belong to a simpler worship. And Slaidburn has never thought fit to change its ways.

On Sunday the congregation fills narrow, high-backed, "sit-up-and-beg" benches in the nave, though many handsome seventeenth-century box pews with farm and family names carved on their doors, and older Jacobean pews with carved ends, occupy the rest of the floor space. The Jacobean three-decker pulpit is used as it ought to be; from the bottom deck the clerk leads the responses, from the second the Rector reads the service and from the top, like the captain of his ship, he preaches his sermon.

The chancel screen is most ornate, dark and impressive, a late specimen covered by rich carving; adjoining, the screen of the Hammerton chapel is a contrast, the plain woodwork is twelfth century—possibly the oldest in the church.

Often the Rector shows other possessions to those who are interested. Have you ever seen the short-handled, leather-thonged dog whips with which the official dog whippers of bygone days were provided? Slaidburn has two, used to clear the church of fighting dogs in the days when farmers brought their four-legged friends to matins with them.

The communion plate is dated 1678 and beautiful in design it is, chalices and patens fitting into each other. The maker is said to have come to a bad end; he was hanged for coin clipping!

If you see purposeful menfolk advancing on the church with ladders and carpet beaters some Monday in Spring watch awhile and you will see mats, carpets, hassocks, carried into the churchyard and a great shaking and batting going on. Inside more will be performing acrobatic feats, brushing away the dust and cobwebs from roof and beams. Tuesday will show "follow-on" activity; regiments of women go to the attack with mops and buckets and brushes, scrubbing, polishing, blackleading pipes, brightening up brass. Gangs carrying baskets and trays, flasks and pots, come to the aid of the work parties with pies, sandwiches and coffee. Spring cleaning!

Some day after farmers have done with haytiming there will be scythes sweeping through the churchyard grass and the quiet graves and table-top tombs will appear again from their meadow grasses and midsummer flowers.

The most picturesque of village schools stands over the church-yard wall, a grammar school founded in 1717 by "John Brennand of Pain Hill, Gentleman", its door handsome in the best early Georgian tradition, the schoolroom lit by high transomed windows.

Everything in the village is in keeping, unassuming, uncluttered, solidly built to last—as we trust it will—for Slaidburn in its entirety is scheduled for preservation, which means no isolated property owner or speculative builder will ever be allowed to spoil what is perfect.

This is a T-shaped village, the street beyond St. Andrew's and school—flanked by rows of cottages with pebbled frontages and tiny under-window garden plots—forking left down Chapel Street to the Hodder, and right, uphill towards Shay Wood and Ellerbeck.

Once two inns occupied the focal point: the Dog faced the Bull. The Black Bull for nearly thirty years has been a very active youth hostel, called King's House because of the squire whose name, King-Wilkinson, is derived from that of the old landowning family. The Dog, its full name "Hark to Bounty", has a long and colourful story and is still going strong.

Long ago the tenants of the Forest came to the Slaidburn court-house to pay their rents for their manors—Knolls of Knowlmere, twelve barbed arrows, the lords of Battersby (Dunnow) one pair of spurs and one barbed arrow—or to take part in Forest courts. An upper room in the inn is still shown where prisoners were tried and sentenced. This court room is of ample dimensions, under heavy rafters sound enough to allow a sheepstealer to be hanged therefrom, with high-backed benches, a wooden-walled dock, witness box, and in the dark wainscotting a door which it is said was opened so that the prisoner could be pushed through into a lock-up.

The curious inn name? Bounty was leader of a full-throated pack of hounds. "Hark to Bounty!" the huntsman cried.

Among the prettiest houses in the village none are prettier than those at the brook side. I stayed in one after a March evening meeting of the W.I. and when I woke was sure it was a rainy morning.

It was the voice of Croasdale Brook a few yards below my window. It sings the best of lullabies and gives a morning reveille blended with the song of birds.

Rising early an earlier riser is startled, a heron fishing, a king-fisher or the cheerful rotund dipper, its voice clear as tinkling water-drops. A robin trills over the crocuses. Starlings tune up on chimney pots waiting for the warmth from smoke of new-lit fires.

Before breakfast I was out on a green bank picking snowdrops, returning by the water mill which for centuries provided power for local needs. It ground local-grown corn; a century ago, in one Winter, five hundred packs, with two hundred and forty pounds to a pack, were ground for local use. Now the clacketty wheel has gone, but the mill pond remains, the weir and three pairs of disused millstones.

There is a thrill about an old mill stirring to life, even when it is a

modern water-turbine bringing machinery into action and with its
" 4,000 revs. a minute" making the whole fabric shiver and shake.

Before leaving Slaidburn, take a walk up the village street, past
Rock House, where the squire lives, to Shay Wood with its carpet of
flowers—dog's mercury and enchanter's nightshade, bluebells and
ransoms—and ceiling of interlaced boughs and foliage. The path is
near the brook and its wall of rock; it passes into a pasture and
climbs to Ellerbeck Hall, a typical Bowland farm of the seventeenth
century. Go on, if you must, to the inviting fells and discover Croasdale and the Hornby road.

HAMMERTON AND DALE HEAD

A family which left its mark on the Hodder valley was the Hammertons, who lived at Hammerton Hall on the river bank as long
ago as the thirteenth century.

They made gifts to the church: Stephen gave the monks of
Kirkstall twenty loads of hay each year, his brother Nicholas
granted land at Cheetall near Clitheroe "To God, St. Nicholas and
the House of Edisford for the leprous brethren there—", and others
helped in the rebuilding of their parish church. But they had a fair
share of black sheep, kinsfolk who were riotous, belligerent, given
to feuds. As late as Tudor times one was outlawed after murdering
Ralph Parker, a neighbour, but after receiving the King's pardon
he settled down, peacefully we trust, on his home ground.

North of the Hall the reservoir dam is a grass-covered wall across
the dale. The Fylde wanted water for summer visitors—so the ancient
manor of Rushton, better known as Dale Head, was drowned—and
a whole community disappeared.

From an old Dale Header I heard what life was like in this backwater, eighty to ninety years ago.

He talked of work and play, especially of the year's highlights,
Christmas and Stocks Sports in June.

One Christmas Eve the carol singers sallied forth from the
"Public", duly fortified, for their night's journey took them from
Brig'house to Swinshaw, Birch Hill to Asker Hill—where all imbibed
from a bowl filled with whisky, rum and gin—before trudging in
the frosty night to New House, Kenibus and to Lamb Hill. Here
there was singing and melodeon playing till 1 a.m., when the
servant girl came down to make a feed for all, and on went the merriment until five in the morning! Then, after the playing of "Bluebells of Scotland" on a concertina, all proceeded to Merrybent Hill—
and home-brewed ale. In the dark, one walked into the "muck
midden". Six a.m. found them still merry at New House. All arrived

home to cope with the morning milking. No lying abed to recover!

Sports: the lads raced from Gammas Field, site of the school, over the Hodder, up "Th' Aik Hills" and back again. They pole-jumped, wrestled and danced lancers and quadrilles to the sound of Slaidburn or Bentham brass band conveyed hither by waggonette, whilst the elders indulged in shag-smoking competitions from clay pipes.

For the children was the Walking from The Field to the strains of "Hail Smiling Morn" from four leading bandsmen. How the day smiled! They visited house and farm in turn, receiving small gifts from each. Swinshaw filled hands with sweets and the Vicarage too; apple and orange for each at Chapel House and at the Grange more sweets. Jenny Simpson doled out toffee sticks, and Bridge House fruit or a penny, whilst the "Public" was ready with nuts. Then weary feet, urged on by thought of a Grand Tea, trudged back to the school. Happy days!

The Vicar was the presiding spirit of the place. He wore clogs, with clasps, blackened so that they shone like silver. He taught the young folk scripture—hour-long sessions—with a cane at the ready, four feet long, and his coat tails to the schoolroom fire. Once they caught alight and fell off! When children used "bad words" he made them drink soapsuds.

Soon there will be no one alive who can bring old Stocks to life. Gone, like "the Kerry dancing and the lilt of the piper's tune", are the jolly days, the red-faced bandsmen, and upstanding young farmers' boys who could walk the farm fence, gathering sheep from snowdrifts, struggle long miles up to the knees in snow, then—not to disappoint a sweetheart—cover twelve miles to a Paythorne rendezvous—"and she didn't turn up!"

Food was wholesome but monotonous. Breakfast, "always porridge with milk, oatcake and bread"; dinner, "fried bacon, taties, and one piece of pie—nothing but rhubarb". But there was the "forenoon drinking", a meal in itself—fat bacon collops, and crisped oatcake made on a backstone and hung to dry on a bread fleak. Tea was drunk only at tea time. Christmas brought a rare treat—"Allus flour podditch, currant loaf for Christmas day in t'morning". After goose killing they lived on giblets for a fortnight!

In that driest of Summers, 1959, I stood on the almost dry bed of the reservoir, on the stones of the bridge beneath which the Hodder was but a yard-wide trickle. A pile of roofing slates, stripped from a riverbank house, remained as the demolition squads had left them. I brought back a few for my garden paving—reminder of what is past and gone.

MIDNIGHT AT DALE HEAD

"Setting out on an all-night walk!" As we left them at Copy Nook the passengers in the Clitheroe to Bolton-by-Bowland bus obviously thought us slightly mad. We feel it too—very slightly, but the feeling soon passes.

From Holden Clough to Anna Lane Head and Threap Green the sun was a dazzle in our eyes; it made of buttercup fields a brighter gold and shone back from farm walls and cottage windows. When the sun dipped at 9.40 behind Burn Moor and Croasdale, red rays radiated from the disappearing orb and flame ran across the sky. At first the fells were pale and insubstantial against the fire of it; as the fire paled to rose and dimmed to pearl so did the fells grow darker until they were indigo silhouettes. That was at 10.30 p.m.

We had reached the Dale Head cross roads. The heavens were still full of lark song—a last frenzy of sound. Curlews called too; they never rest but watchers cry in the night—late and early. Then the owls began their hunting over the pines of Gisburn Forest. Wild duck flew in pairs towards the gleaming waters of the Stocks reservoir.

Night was near, coming "in mantle grey—star inwrought".

There is no dead of night in June. At 11 p.m. when we found a dry and soft bed beneath the pines near the water edge the silence was full of small sounds; owls, curlews and constant bickering of water fowl. Outside the pines white mist wraiths crawled over the lakes, but nothing dimmed the stars.

We allowed ourselves two hours rest.

Out of the silence a bird "wound-up"—a whirring nightjar in the pine trees! The night became full of small sounds—from the lake with its summer population of mallard and tufted duck, teal and pochard. An occasional sweet call came from the sky: small snuffles and flutterings from the water edge.

At 1.15 we stirred ourselves, stood up beneath the sheltering pines, watched the Great Bear sprawling across the western heavens. Then, a bright light shone behind us, the suddenly appearing moon which we had written off as a non-player during our night's walk. It lit up the next three miles, it shone with preternatural light on the banks of white mist shrouding the lake—it whitened our road and wayside trees threw strange shadows.

One of the embarrassing features of an all-night walk is the drawing up of night-riders offering lifts which we have no desire to accept. About 1.30 a large car drew up, the headlights of which had flashed behind, in the valley, warning us of its approach. I wonder what the driver thought as he drove on, his offer rejected. "We are walk-

ing for the pleasure of it," we said, "strange though it may seem."
It was too dark to read the expression on his face. His voice sounded
incredulous.

We were to be passed by no other night riders, for which we were
most thankful.

Silently we climbed to the skyline and waited by the wall and the
gate. Knotts in Bowland at last. At 2.30 the first bird called, a lark
rose from the dark earth then more followed and a score of larks were
singing from the sky, invisible voices. Then a curlew cried—once.

Day was breaking over Craven and rosy tints running across the
sky. At 3.30 a moorcock rose and called, and a cuckoo shouted.
Grouse in families began to gossip and grumble among heather
tussocks; a cock talked to his mate in voice almost human, "Come
out, now, now, now—come out". The east was throbbing with
light and colour, but behind us it was still shrouded in night.

We walked into enchantment. At 4 o'clock Keasden showed every
stick, stone and tree in its true colour, the blossom on rowan and
hawthorn, the many greens of oak and ash and farm sycamores.

For an hour the flocks had been feeding at the roadside; daybreak,
dawn and sunrise are all one to them. No farm had made any comment by 4.30; the Keasden farms all slept on. Not until 5.50, descending field tracks from Long Bank and Coppy Close, did we see the
first sign of activity; there was a stampede of cows with dog at heels
and a rush to a farm gate where a man was calling them up for
milking.

At 6.30 we hit the hard highroad near Harden Bridge and Austwick. The day had really begun and traffic throbbed by, from Leeds—
Lancaster—Kendal—north and east!

If you have never ranged the Lamb Hill Fell and Bowland Knotts
skyline, nor been thrilled by the quite sensational views therefrom,
you have missed a rare experience. Always lovely—when the
Craven tops are snow-capped, when the March winds blow, when
Autumn riots over the heather slopes and whin-cushioned heights,
it is perhaps best when heather and ling are in full bloom and ripe
whinberries are ready for the picking.

ON MARL HILL—A FELL ROAD

A sudden little lane "that curls and climbs elusive to a sky of
dreams", that is the Marl Hill road on a pale blurred morning in
early Autumn before the thin mists have been swept aside by the
sun. I love it then above all times though others declare—"Oh,
Barney Brow in May", or "Wait till all the leaves have turned;
then it is a picture."

For me there is no off-season, though I confess the heathery acres of Birkett Fell when crimson in September, and the smooth limestone pastures of Radholme Laund or the green intakes behind Ashknott in cuckoo time with many lambs calling tremolo and ewes answering mezzo-soprano, and October when the pheasant flies heavy over the wild cherry trees and the beeches of Cragstones Wood and shares in the same rich colouring, are much to my liking.

Interested in rocks and stones? Then the very walls dividing the fells and hollows will prove interesting. The gritstone walls at Cow Ark become speckled with white limestone; at higher level, at Radholme Laund, they are limestone with only gritstone as "throughs". Notice how the corner stones, window jambs and doorposts of wayside farms, and the walls of some, are a pinky, rosy-tinted freestone rarely seen in these parts. Ask any local farmer and he will direct you to the quarries upon Kitcham and Birkett from which their building stone was taken.

On the fell top between Marl Hill and the Waddington Fell skyline at Walloper Well are the sphinx-like Cragstones, huge outcrops of rock. The rough pastures sweep down to Ashknott and all the soothing contrast of sheep-bitten pastures, old limestone quarry and lime kilns. There the knowledgeable seek the dark holes which are found at close quarters to be the shafts of eighteenth-century lead mines.

If history is more to your taste than geology, then think of the Romans who, for three centuries, trod the same hillways en route from Ribchester northwards to The Wall; from Bateson's farm their road strikes over rough ground and above Crimptons brook, reaching the Hodder levels at last, south of Newton Bridge.

Foulscales at the brow foot is as old as it looks, the oldest farm on Knowlmere estate. The walls are of tremendous thickness, its doors have well-shaped mouldings, the small windows admit far more light than looks possible; outside stone steps are far older than its indoor staircases and the massive chimney projecting from one gable older than those on the roof line. The odd projection on the south end was in fact a mod. con. of olden times; "Like a throne over a chute," is the farmer's comment.

He adds, "Monks stayed here when Slaidburn church was being built." Probably it acted as a fourteenth-century hospice.

Its neighbour across the brook is Storths, a fine house dismantled when the Parkers no longer needed it. Its classical door graces the next farm, Longstripes, where one evening Mr. Pinder, whose forbears have long lived hereabouts, blew the "view halloo" on a long brass hunting horn, inscribed C. R. Parker 1800, for my diversion.

The horn had been given to a former Pinder, huntsman to the Parkers.

No Bowland farmer is too busy to indulge in a "bit of a crack". I remember standing and staring with a cowhand at Birkett, both of us considering the croonings and pawings of the bull. We looked at large patches of earth his pawings had bared. "Well," he said, scratching his head, "when it's gone and bared this'n we'll have to put bull ower yon in that'n," and he indicated another small walled-in field.

We talk of common land and the unstinted pasture of Newton Fell where there is no limit to the number of sheep turned out. One farmer says, "My sheep winter and summer it up there. Mine are heafed sheep, lambed and sucked on't' fell."

In February a farm lad reports, "At daybreak I heard first curlew —in half song," and we know Spring is on its way.

Six weeks later the farmer looking to his lambing ewes on a high meadow comments, "It were a grand night, dampish, but it was good to hear flocks of curlew whistling over."

Soon it will be a report of the first cuckoo and the return of the swallows.

On Marl Hill we drink in the beauty of a summer day and gaze our fill of the heavenly circle of mountains and fells.

"There's no bonnier sight," reflects the countryman, "but time I like best is August, and heather in full bloom. Then when I open my door to look out, how the scent rushes in!"

"THE TROUGH"—A BOWLAND PASS

There used to be a time when to cross the Bowland boundary by The Trough was considered an act of "derring-do". A traveller who said, "I've just come through The Trough," was looked at as if he had crossed the Khyber Pass without falling into the hands of brigands, or come through the St. Bernard Pass without being rescued by the dogs.

What changes now! Cars mount the coiling ascent to The Trough Stone without mishap. They rattle over the cattle grids which have replaced the gates where tramps held out grimy hands, or the old man at Keeper's Cottage collected pennies in aid of Blackburn Royal Infirmary. So many picnickers pull up on the level ground near Sykes that sheep, having been fed so often, make themselves a nuisance to anyone who stops there.

No longer need one take the road from Lancaster to Whalley or Clitheroe fearing he might succumb to hunger or privation en route; hot coffee and sandwiches and ice-cream in the summer—

kiosks provide them at strategic points. Take the road any fine day in July or August and it will be picnicking, picnicking all the way— tables put up, spirit stoves lit, kettles boiling, deck chairs in place, radios blaring——

The Trough has always been popular, but never so much as now. It has been "discovered" with a vengeance.

But it is still the most dramatic fell crossing, especially at quiet times when you can well imagine the fears which overtook travellers benighted—or apprehensive of footpads—or caught in gales or

"The Trough" near Sykes

blizzards. Long miles still divide Dunsop Bridge and Staple Oak from Sykes, and Sykes from Marshaw, and night is just as dark as in the old days, and loneliness weighs down the spirits of the lone wayfarer in the 1960s just as in the 1460s.

What exactly is The Trough?

It is not the whole of Bowland but the pass only—from Sykes to Marshaw—with Whins Brow and Top O'Blaze Moss hemming it in. At the watershed The Trough Stone was the forest boundary between Wyresdale and Bowland, and when the county of Lancaster was created and the whole of Bowland remained in Yorkshire, it marked the border of the two shires also.

In spite of the wild region encompassing it, The Trough road was always well used, by men on Forest and Duchy business, by traders bound to Clitheroe from Lancaster, by humble travellers making their way from abbey to abbey where free hospitality was to be had, and in troubled times by armed men. The Scots found it a convenient inroad when they swept south on hit-and-run raids. In the Civil War both sides used it on cross-country sorties.

What drama one can imagine enacted between the glowering fells! My only attempt at novel writing stopped short at the rescue of a young and beautiful Lancashire witch (innocent, of course) by her lover who waited, in hiding, by the bridge near Sykes; the get-away was to have been by Langden Castle and Fiendsdale.

Very old Clitheronians told tales of "walking through t'Trough to hangings at Lancaster". Once Gallows Corner drew crowds to the castle when sentences were carried out in view of the public. Our parents remembered The Trough road, the white dust, the loose stones—and inevitable punctured wheels.

I remember the brown brooks flowing out of Harden and Langden, the bright water down in the dale reflecting the sky and a-dazzle in the sunshine, merry little streams chuckling through bracken and heather, waterfalls leaping over rocks beneath rowans—and the green trees around Sykes farm and tiny, precious, green meadow land intaken from the hills, and lonely farms perched high and almost out of sight, where old folk watched the traffic, and cars, like toys, move along the grey road far and away below—and where a farm wife laughed at the idea of feeling lonely, "Lonely—no, I never feel lonely. You see, there are the trees, and trees are that good company."

I remember a midsummer night spent on the hills overlooking The Trough road and coming from the silent tops to the hard road just before dawn and, where the hills drew nearer together like huge, black, sleeping beasts, one bird flying over and calling—once. That curlew's cry over The Trough will be with me all my life.

Everyone passing through catches some such moment of haunting loveliness. Maybe it is a sunset touch over Lonsdale and Morecambe Bay; maybe a touch of fiery splendour on an Autumn day, or green fire—and cuckoos calling—in Spring; or a remembered family picnic —or the day you shared with a well-loved friend.

Walkers Only

WHITENDALE AND BRENNAND

Only walkers can penetrate to the deep heart of Bowland, into the secret recesses of Whitendale and Brennand, which retained their Forest character long after the rest was "civilized" farmland. When Nicholas Assheton wrote in his 1617 journal—"To Batterise—to Burn Side and Whitendale, overrun with good deer", game was already scarce in other parts of Bowland.

Middle Knoll separates Whitendale and Brennand

A rough track makes from Dunsop post office[1] up the level holms of the Dunsop River valley to Holm Head cottages, on to Bishops farm and the plot of land called Foot Holm, where the two smaller dales meet below the round shoulders of Middle Knoll.

For the first three miles the high fells, Staple Oak and Beatrix, have held back, kept their distance, but now only the aggressive thrusting Knoll seems to be holding them at bay. What a fine sight it is, raked by prowling cloud shadows, curlews crying over it and the shy ring ousel's sweet call over the whins!

[1] Walkers take Hodder bus to this point. Motorists who wish to explore the dales leave their cars here.

Birdsong, the wind's voice, the sound of blown waters—no other company but one's own thoughts until one or other of the farms is reached. To Whitendale it is an up-and-down route before dropping into a tiny green oasis in mid-dale, where grey houses cluster by the river and one tremendous sky-reaching ash tree—the biggest in Bowland—has an odd companion, a tall monkey puzzle tree.

In Forest days a keeper lived here; modern keepers have kept down vermin in a different way, waging war on rodents, moles, ravens, stoats and weasels and the black-backed gull, which they exhibited on a fence "gallows".

There are two ways out; following the stream to the wild fells, Shooter's Clough and the Roman road above Croasdale, or steeply up the fell behind the farm, above Calf Clough to black peat haggs floored with silver sand, and over the tops where small pools mirror the sky and attract gulls to the nesting ground on their verge in Spring. Both routes make eastwards towards Slaidburn.

Brennand House is the only farm in the twin dale, low-lying with a fantastic pattern of fields and intake walls on the valley floor, and bare treeless slopes rising from its gates. Its skyline runs along the county boundary, on the tops of Whins Brow, Brennand Great Hill, Threaphaw Fell and Wolfhole Crag.

Long ago, forest folk found a short cut into Wyresdale by Millers House. Often we have scrambled up a steep ravine to the heights by Brennand farm, there to descend to Wyresdale Tower "site" and The Trough road near Marshaw. The best outlet is from the farm's back gate, by an ancient path called Ouster Rake which climbs to the peaty tops of Whins Fell, two exhilarating miles. If the path peters out—not to worry—for, the day being clear, the deep defile of The Trough can be seen over to the west. We drop to the pasture walls, down to Trough House farm from which a track takes us down again by Ramsclough to the highway near Sykes.

Bowland is criss-crossed by similar high fell routes first used by forest dwellers. One short-cut—from The Trough road at Sykes into Bleasdale and Chipping—is more exciting than any other I know, but to be avoided in storm or hill mist.

OVER THE TOPS—SYKES TO BLEASDALE

At Langden Brook, near Sykes, no one would guess—being sur-rounded by picnickers, paddlers, idlers and ice-cream lickers—that down the valley beyond the plantations and Preston W.W. buildings is the loneliest and wildest corner of Bowland.

Half a mile updale, the river twisting and turning in its stony bed, every bend opening out new unexpected landscapes, is part of a land of complete solitude. At the barn—Langden Castle on maps—the track is less clear, the going spongy, the dale more constricted. Many gullies bring down cascading streams; one is Bleadale, another Fiendsdale, the two divided by the interposing Nab.

The Langden Water is forded as best we can, the toiling path climbed as it loops the fellside facing the Nab—a squelchy path we once trod barefoot carrying sodden footwear—until at 1,400 feet we are above the world, ringed round by a vast Homeric sea of high fells, wave beyond wave of blue, purple, indigo.

These are heady heights; we stand and declaim the names of the familiar hills—a noble-sounding roll call—from the Craven mountains shouldering away the sky, to the little hillocks of the Fylde. The sea is away over the plains, a gleaming silvery expanse, and more often than not it is a good spanking sea breeze which races across the tops.

The tops themselves; not a good place to be when mists gather or night is coming on. Attempt the crossing only with many hours of daylight in hand, for the bogs are vast and after a rainy season only the stakes give the wanderer a feeling of security as he plods from one to another.

Naturally this is wet going; scores of springs rise here and the Calder, the Brock and many lesser streams take their waters from this vast sponge. The county boundary, reeling like a drunkard hopelessly lost, crosses Holm House Fell beyond which the way at last takes on the look of the bridle track is really is.

Like a wide ribbon it is thrown down the slope, to the first farms of the Bleasdale rim. Old homesteads, small green intakes, farmyard noises, children's voices—all the kindly sounds of the "civilized" countryside are about us now.

A track direct from Holm House heads to Admarsh church, Bleasdale and the Brock byways to Garstang and A6. A roundabout way, farm to farm, links Holm House with Higher Fairsnape, Blindhurst, Higher Core, and hugging the foot of Parlick Pike all lanes lead to Chipping.

From Sykes in The Trough to Bleasdale hamlet—6½ miles.

Chipping is 4 miles farther on—by lanes.

FOOTPATHS IN BOWLAND

"Nature and the countryside will not confide their secrets to a man in a hurry. Man was born a pedestrian——"

With an inch-to-the-mile Ordnance Survey map, Sheet 95, take to the field paths along the Hodder and over the fells, "hide your cycle in the bracken" or leave your car at the roadside, and stride out a free man.

From Clitheroe to Newton Bridge or Dunsop (9 miles).

Over Edisford bridge follow the Whitewell road, find the path to Cheetall farm and on to Bashall Hall, Cow Hey and Saddle Bridge, an ancient track to Browsholme by brook, through meadows, along a lane through the Bashall Moor plantations. Behind the second Hall lodge a path rises up rough pastures to Spire farm, reaching the top of Marl Hill. The route is down to Foulscales, across two fields to the Hodder bank at Newton Bridge.

From Foulscales and Farrowfield walkers may use the drive through Knowlmere park, following it as far as Mossthwaite farm, where a stiled path makes for the river side, against the walls of Thorneyholme. Dunsop is over the footbridge.

From Clitheroe over Waddington Fell to Slaidburn (9 miles).

A stiled path from Brungerley farm gate (over the bridge) goes over pastures to West Bradford bridge and the village. Eaves Hall lane climbs past a new caravan site on once-wooded ground—it is called Three Rivers, the title of my first book, but I had no hand in the naming—and finally, above the tree belt, becomes a rough track leaving farmland for high fell, then a wandering path with barking grouse and great space. In the one wall straddling the tops is Chatburn Nook stile, from which glorious views and more to come. Ahead is the fell road at Walloper Well; we turn right over the heather to strike the Easington Fell track which drops to a fell-foot farm, crosses quiet pastures to Skelshaw farm and after using a footbridge over Easington Brook forges straight ahead, tops a hill ridge. Not far beyond and below is the Hodder, Slaidburn bridge and the village, an unexpected picture which in the hush of an April evening—or any other time—catches at the heartstrings.

Hodder Bank Paths from Whitewell to Burholme Bridge and Stocks.

This is a pleasant walk for anyone leaving the bus at Whitewell, or the car at Burholme Bridge, arranging to be picked up at Slaidburn.

A mile beyond Whitewell hotel we come to Burholme bridge and take the farm track from the gate to the huddle of grey buildings ahead, the old farm group. Over the footbridge we keep close to the river all the way to Root footbridge and Thorneyholme, where we come to the second "meeting of the waters". We have seen Langden Brook join the Hodder; here the Dunsop river flows down to meet her. Over the footbridge an avenue flanked by giant Wellingtonia Sequoias leads to Dunsop.

If we do not cross the bridge over the Hodder we may follow the riverside—scent of Sweet Cicily in Summer and golden leaves of beeches an Autumn glory—mount the pastures to Mossthwaite and take Knowlmere manor drive to Farrowfield and field paths again to Newton Bridge. Crossing the river we find an invitation to make use of a lovely path, first over a stone causeway smothered in water plants, then along the Hodder bank to Dunnow Hall. Just beyond we come to the road and Slaidburn church has a welcoming look.

North of Slaidburn; my favourite path begins at the Hodder bridge and, from stile to stile, finds the elysian fields of Bell Sykes, loitering between margins and drifts of meadow flowers. It is paved part of the way. Holme Head bridge is not far off, reflected beautifully in the Hodder, and Hammerton Hall looks down the dale.

Here the persistent walker may find paths through the new "forest" to the "new" Dale Head church. The reservoir and the drowned valley fill the country beyond.

Little Bowland and the Park of Leagram

Here we who are Lancastrians can say, "Now we are in our own part of Bowland, though but a small corner of it." This is the 7 square miles cut off by the twelfth-century "boundary commissioners". The Crown always allowed their Master Forester to impark Leagram for his own use though holding on to Little Bowland itself.

Master Foresters' Accounts for 1322 and 1335 give details of the imparking process, this being necessary to confine the deer, improve their feeding grounds for better fattening as venison and to allow more pasture for cattle and horse breeding. Nicholas Swindlehurst did the oak felling and timber splitting to make the palings and rails, whilst Henry Pemberton dug 67 roods of new ditch, 8 feet wide and 4½ deep, easily leapt by deer without the Pale but confining them once they had sampled the herbage within. Triple rows of whitethorns planted on the bank completed the 5-mile fence.

Walking from Leagram and Chipping towards Lickhurst and the fells, look for traces of this bank and ditch. Names give a clue; Fence and Fence Wood, Pale Farm, Park Stile, Parkgate. And there is a Buck Banks.

The Lodge, later site for Leagram Hall, belonged to the deputy keepers who overlooked the Park for the Master Foresters—these being non-residents such as Earls of Shrewsbury, Lords Clifford, Stanleys and Monteagles—collected revenues for "gisting", the letting of grazing rights within the Park to cattle owners who had insufficient feed, summering or wintering, for their cattle.

The royal herds were "gisted" too, free of course, but to others the charges were—for wintering on Fence pastures and for summering or wintering within the Park, oxen and bullocks—9d. and 18d. a head.

As in Pendle, Henry VII decided on changes. He leased and farmed out the Park to Hoghtons and Sherburnes, keen rivals when in or out of office, keepers or poachers accordingly. Elizabeth went further and gave orders to dis-park. Leagram was bought then by the Sherburnes, who made The Lodge their home, a timber-built, rush-thatched and wattle-and-daub-walled building; in the eighteenth century their descendants, the Welds, rebuilt it, but this Hall has in recent years been dismantled. Only the site is left.

The best English landscape has on it the hand of Man co-operating with Nature; so in Little Bowland, where for generations the Welds worked upon a landscape they found neglected and wild. When they inherited it was a "lost Land" without any road better than bridle and cattle tracks, with no bridges over its rivers, and barriers keeping out any stranger who thought to cross the country. They raised funds for rebuilding the old Doeford bridge destroyed by Hodder floods in 1770—when tragedy hit a bridal party here—and new bridges over Loud were erected in 1835. New farms were built, farmers encouraged to try dairy farming on a better scale, discouraged to put their trust in success of corn growing, for only precarious oat crops ever ripened hereabouts. Of the timber only Forest left-overs—dwarf oaks, birch, hollies and alders—grew, so large-scale tree planting was begun.

From all this we benefit. Little Bowland is a small Paradise—fresh, clean, breeze-swept country—just what the walker likes best.

For walkers; two ancient tracks are worth taking. One from the north side of Doeford bridge crosses the fields to the seventeenth-century farmhouse called Stakes, which stands at the Hodder brink. When the river is low, stepping stones can be crossed and the way continued on the "common passage from Wardsleys to Farrick House Pasture (Fair Oak), Connerie Close and Farrick House Fold, thereafter by way of a close called Highfield through Long Knott to New Lawnes". This is a path over the limestone pastures above the Hodder cliffs and the Fairy Hole Caves near Whitewell.

The other track, centuries old and still used by local farmers as a short-cut to The Trough of Bowland and Wyresdale, crosses Leagram and makes for Bleasdale and the Langden valley. This route, in reverse, is given as "Sykes to Bleasdale", on page 139.

LITTLE BOWLAND BYWAYS

Roads enter Little Bowland at three points only, from Burholme Bridge near Whitewell, from Loud Mytham Bridge near Doeford, and from Chipping via Leagram. Intended only for the farming folk they are narrow and need care in the "narrows". Park the car as soon as possible and find your greater pleasure on foot; the path-finder is best rewarded.

The road route; Burholme, by Fair Oak House, the unfenced road over Greystoneley pastures, to Doeford, 4½ miles; to Chipping, 5½ miles. On foot, leave this byway, on discovery bent, at three points.

One mile above Burholme Bridge a stony track heads away to the fells, through Tunstall Ing farmyard and on into complete seclusion —and to Whitmore, surely one of Lancashire's loneliest farms, a relic of Forest days, gripping the fell with unshaking tenacity. Back to Tunstall Ing, climb to the "slackest part o' th' hill", a gentle saddle on the ridge, lean back on the wind, get your balance, and gaze your fill. That knot of grey farms below is Dinkling Green.

Winter paints the landscape in dark, sombre hues; in the wind you imagine the huntsman's horn and the belling of hounds. But in May and June; then you can well believe in fairies—if you have time for whimsey, or are under seven—as you sit in the snowfall of a haw-thorn tree with a cuckoo calling and curlews crying, or tread the thyme-scented, close-bitten turf. They believed in fairies once, those dwellers in Dinkling Green, whose forbears had kept the royal beasts in the gentle sun-drenched hollow, and gathered them into secure folds when wolves ranged the fells.

The second track leaves the road near Fair Oak House; through a gate and round a bend—another bewitching glimpse of Dinkling Green. Go forward to the clustering buildings; there behind the farmyard follow a rough track to the left, over a rounded hill, and in less than a mile you will be looking across a dell—with a com-plicated system of water splashes and fords, to the high-standing Lickhurst farms.

Lickhurst, a group of seventeenth-century farms, is another reminder of the days when Forest tenants were becoming yeoman farmers, building their new homes on sites of earlier vaccaries. The Park pale is not far below, where sun-drenched fields—this fell slope gets all the sun that is going, it is the bright hillside we can see from far away in Ribblesdale—dip to Buckbank Wood and a path, a short-cut to Chipping, runs away to Park Stile and Leagram. Another path goes over the bare fell called Stanley, behind Lickhurst, coming to the fords of Burnslack Brook and winding lanes to Chipping Brook, exhilarating walking especially when the heather is in bloom.

Leaving the car by the telephone kiosk near Fair Oak farm you may explore from the three ways meeting here, Dinkling Green through the gate ahead and Lickhurst by taking the lane to the left and over the fords.

From the head of Chipping Brook track down the most exciting under-fell farm, Wolfen Hall, locally "Wo'of House", remote from any other haunt or dwelling, where early Chepyns, Knolls and Sherburnes lived—some as wild as the hills about them—poachers of the king's deer, harbourers of wanted men, themselves outlawed and forced to hide in their own secret cloughs. Good fighters all of them, springing to arms when called upon—as in Agincourt when,

"The billmen of Bowland, Old Lancashire's pride,
    Stood firm as their hills and the foeman defied."

They were on the spot in 1533 when Roger Sherburne made ready "twenty-four tall men and good archers they being my Lord's (Derbys) tenants, as footmen, to be sent to my Isle (Man) for defence against the Lord of the Outer Isles and sum Scots".

It was said that if the venerable yew at Wolf House gate ever fell that would be the end of the house. It did—in 1952—but to avert the curse a young yew was at once planted within the roots of the old.

In midwinter, when every thorn crouches, writhen, twisted, against the blast and the very fells draw up their knees against the cold, think of the men who kept watch here, ready to cry "Wolf" when the grey predatory beasts came down upon vaccary and fold.

CHIPPING VILLAGE

No one should leave this countryside without visiting Chipping, for centuries its heart and soul.

You fall in love with it at once, such a snug, close-packed, self-contained and friendly place it is. Its narrow streets are flanked by seventeenth- and eighteenth-century cottages and the several inns—letting you know it was always a meeting place for travellers—are of the good old unpretentious kind which fit best into a village scene. To make the picture quite perfect, the church looks down on all, like a mother over her children.

First glances might give a false impression that Time has stood still—or turned back into itself. Chippings should be market towns. This was in the Middle Ages, disposing of the surplus of farms and vaccaries in Chippingdale; no obvious trading goes on now, no blatant signs of industry.

Until a century ago Chipping Brook turned the wheels of five mills. And now? Five "mills" still at work but none dependent on water wheels. You need to search for them, for Chipping in the last two decades has wooed industry without losing her rural charm. Tucked away in a wooded clough are two factories, each over a century old and growing with the years. One is the Kirk Chair factory producing fine reproduction and modern chairs and the other the Tweedy Foundry which, in its time, has turned out iron and brass wares as diverse as ships' rudders, wheels and portholes, to chip machine and "crisp" slicers and dehydrators. Enlarged beyond recognition they both bring in employees by the bus load. Smaller concerns, where old mills once turned, are a corn mill for cattle and poultry food and two creameries and cheese factories.

The church, an older daughter of Whalley, has an aged yew to the east contemporary or older than the first building which was

Brabbin School and Almshouses, Chipping

added to in the fourteenth century. I like the portraits of village artisans carved on a north arcade pillar, and the touching wall brass in the chancel, a memorial to the two wives of Robert Parkinson of Fairsnape, a seventeenth-century piece.

Modern craftsmanship in the ancient church is in the wood-carving of choir stalls by a worker at the chair mill, and the wrought-iron grille by the vestry from the hand of a foundry worker.

If you talk to an old native he will possibly tell you of Chipping's old-time fairs, festivals and jollifications which seem to have made the year a round of activity mixed with merriment.

One will direct your attention to a cottage by the Post Office where John Brabbin was born; he was the founder of the attractive Bluecoat

School in Windy Street with its dated porch (1684), and of the adjoining almshouses. There is an old well down a flight of steps hollowed with three centuries of use, and a handrail worn smooth by old hands.

You will hear the sad tale of the Sun Inn maid who wakened on her wedding morn, her heart " like a singing bird ", looked from her chamber window to the church porch—and saw there her faithless bridegroom leaving with another woman on his arm. It makes a good story, and is quite true. All the ingredients of Victorian melodrama are in it, including a curse " which came true ", and suicide.

It used to be said, " It cuckoos all winter i' Chipping ", a reference to the tale of simple villagers who once thought to wall in the cuckoo and so keep perpetual spring. " They say " Chippingers had only one knife at one period and a cry " Whittle to t' tree ! " brought out the last borrower, to hand over.

ROADS THROUGH CHIPPINGDALE

(1) From Longridge town, to Tootill Heights, down Birks Brow to Wheatley's winding lanes, out at Thornley school and so into Hesketh lane. Here two ways lead into Chipping, the first by Goose Lane and the second by Daub Hall. From the Dog and Partridge, walk along the farm lane on the left to the Tudor house of Hesketh End with extraordinary carved lettering on its walls, a history of England from BRUTUS · ERECTUS · LONDINV · ANTE-CHRIST · 108 · to ANGLIA CONQUER · FLODDAN · 1513.

(2) From Longridge town and the Derby Arms, Thornley, strike away on bylanes hithering and thithering to Inglewhite—or Parlick Pike and right turns into Chipping.

From the lane to Inglewhite go in search of Ashes farm and White-chapel Church. You might "find yourself lost", and arrive on a Beacon Fell track. A lucky break ! From its summit above the conifers, on foot, you reach a most spectacular viewpoint, all Lancashire spread out like a coloured map. Like Keat's hilltop—on which he stood tip-toe—from Beacon Fell, sky and cloud, hill and dale, acquire a magic to be felt, not spoken of.

Wray: village architecture

11 Hindburn and Roeburn

SOME DAY, BREASTING the last rise of Lamb Hill Fell above the
Hodder source, looking north into Craven, you will say, "There's
wizardry at work".

That is when Ingleborough and all his west-looking brethren are
lined up to advance in strength against Bowland; even the clouds
are in mass formation too, threatening. Then the sun comes out and
the attackers melt away into nothing more than sun gleams and
cloud-laid shadows. This often happens on a Winter day, or with the
vivid theatrical effects of March or November when the whole landscape, clear in every detail, is "magicked" away as at the sweep of a
wand.

Part of this north country is shared by two dales, the Hindburn
below us, and the Roeburn to the west. A charmed region, out of this
world.

The Hindburn

This river begins in fells where the Romans plodded, but their
road has disappeared beneath bog, peat and heather. It comes at
lower level to a dale little visited, almost as Nature left it until below
the farms of Bank End, Lyth and Swans small intakes are defined
and green pastures and emerald mown meadows brighten the brown
and umber slopes.

Each farm is sited in elysian fields, a happy sight dotted with

ewes and lambs in April. Three centuries of wind and rain have
battered their strong walls, greened their stone-flagged roofs, but
so substantial are they all that they seem ready to withstand the
gales of more centuries to come. I like the flourish the stone carvers
gave to the designs on the lintels; a fine textured stone encouraged
them to produce artistic work.

The first hamlet the one dale lane comes to is Ivah, picturesque
in every way, a dream of a place to send town dwellers into ecstasies.
Farther on, Lowgill is more of a village with the Rose and Crown
inn (which has not changed one iota in the twenty years I have
known it) in mid-street, a church and school above a deep ghyll, and
the company of many farms. Nothing, not even the invasion of
labourers for the building of the Haweswater-Manchester pipeline
and tunnels, permanently ruffled its tranquil face. The river hides
shyly, deep in the dale. All farms are sited high above it, with
pastures and meadows below them and wild fells behind them. If
you want to cross the valley to visit one or other take the paths
descending steeply from the Lowgill lane. They lose their way, and
yours; but "not to worry". They peter out in copse and clearings
embroidered with flowers in Spring, deliciously scented, where I am
never in a hurry to leave. There is always a way out to one or other
of the farms, perhaps not the one you set out for. But some farmer
will set you right, from Crag Hall with its Jacobean architecture
and mysterious garden grottoes, or pleasant Park House (1777 on its
date stone) or from Birks with its three building periods, or from
Lower Houses and Over Houses.

All ways, lanes and field paths, come eventually to Wray. There
the Hindburn joins the Roeburn.

Roeburndale

The Roeburn is as hide-away as the Hindburn, at first in deep
cloughs below the farms of Salter (three of them) then disappearing
below Barking Gate into the secret places of Backsbotton where it is
for one mile "wrapped in mystery among rocks impending awfully".
When it comes into the sunlight again, Wray is in sight.

The dale head is known only by walkers, shooting parties, and
foolish motorists who ignore warnings and attempt a track which at
its best is soft peat and at its worst a quagmire. But for walkers able
to foot it lightly in the soft places it is one of the best of fell crossings,
over the Bowland and county boundary on Salter Fell, above Whitendale and Mallowdale.

Nowhere are more splendid prospects, heart-breakingly lovely in
many moods. I remember mad March days with winds piping loud

and every moorbird grounded, when braced against the blast we have marvelled to see a complete magic circle of high fells around us standing their ground without rocking. Still Autumn evenings too, drenched in golden light when distant Lakeland mountains, nearer fells, sea and sky were part of a sunset harmony; not a sound but a solitary homing bird over Mallowdale. And glimmering July days when the fells enclosing Whitendale, Croasdale and the little dale below were only backdrops in monotone, not tangible masses of lime-stone, gritstone, slate.

Dream village—Wray

Wray stands above the meeting of the waters. Its name means an "out of the way corner", which was true when Norse settlers chose to live here. Three roads bring the world into the village now, so it is not isolated or such an odd corner.

The main highway comes in from Hornby and Lancaster by the Lune valley. Down the Wenning from Ingleton, the Benthams and Burton, wanders another lesser highway joined by the fell edge by-ways through Keasdon and Green Smithy, from Clapham and Settle. From the north another road looks in, from Wennington and Tatham. From the south hillmen descend out of the two dales to swell the throng.

But there never is a throng. Wray, like the very best of dream villages, appears to the incomer to be dreaming the happy hours away.

At first glance it is a collection of cottages with pebble "fronts", houses with pebbled paths and strange-shaped stones adorning low garden walls, a shop or two, a street lamp held up by a cherubic figure—and a complete lack of uniformity. It has a wayward, hap-hazard look as of a row of children who will not keep still and toe the line before the race begins. Some houses step back modestly, others push forward to see what is coming down the street; a few turn round with their backs to it, and some hide down narrow yards. One row seems about to slip into the river. The rest are farm-houses with adjoining barns, shippons and stables; they space them-selves out along the street but somehow seem to have no part in it. In the days when milking time saw cows filing sedately down between the houses, and farmer and dog followed behind, farm life flowed down the highway; for the rest of the time activity was con-fined inwards in those cobbled farmyards behind the Tudor and Jacobean walls.

When Wray seems to be having its "forty winks", not a soul stirring, just look behind the nodding houses. You will be surprised to find what goes on in the background. I once found in one yard oak being boiled in preparation for the making of swills—oak spale baskets. Wood working in another form was being done in the wheelwright's—where the main street narrows—and a craft very much practised when half Lancashire was shod in wooden-soled clogs, was still carried on in a yard overlooking the Roeburn banks where I found a clog block maker at work. Wray had its swill maker too, twisting the oak spales, plaiting them in and over a frame of hazel; finished baskets were piled in his workshop.

You may not be lucky enough to find the craftsmen at work; their labour is seasonal, and changes come quickly. Ask any elderly villager about other local industries and possibly you will hear of a nail maker's by the bridge, silk weaving, silk hat making, a wood turner's in a riverside mill, and bobbin making. But the days when the dale rang with sounds of men felling, lopping, singling to provide the raw materials for Wray's former craftsmen are long past.

Take a look at the village store, behind an eighteenth-century bow window, its ceiling supported by the uprights of a four-poster bed; what a fascinating array of goods, which I have known to include rabbit snares and mouse traps, baby food and dog biscuits, caviare, chicken in aspic and *paté de foie gras*, tightly packed on full counter and crowded shelves. It sells "just everything"!

Wander down side lanes and back streets too, un-noticed places where martins feed nestlings and swallows their young in clay daubed nests under barn eaves. Find Dick Brow and the narrow way threading its course round The Spout and Kitty Bridge, "Where they used to drown the kittlings". Then climb up to Outhwaite until the blue mountains of Lakeland appear and every step you take brings in more ridges, peaks and pikes; I walk up backwards way and so enjoy the up as much as the down.

Roaming the surrounding fells Hornby Castle becomes one's lodestone, a landmark rising from the Lune, watching the meeting of many rivers. The Wenning flows by, and the combined waters of Roeburn and Hindburn. It is like a fairy-tale castle come to life.

Hornby Castle

The Norman Montbegons could not have chosen a better place for watching all comers to the fords on the two rivers below their rock. Horni a Viking warrior, Ulf a Danish settler and Romans and Celts had appreciated the site too. Few undesirables could approach without being apprehended.

The castle survived the days of Scots invasion. The Harringtons who were here in the fifteenth century were implicated in the Wars

of the Roses, which led to mustering of local forces at Hornby and
riding forth to battle. When two Harrington heiresses married
Stanleys a new name came on the scene. The Stanley of Marmion's
last cry at Flodden lived here and for his part in leading Lonsdale
and Lancastrian forces at that great victory against the Scots he was
created Lord Monteagle. He built the Monteagle Tower on the
church.

In the Civil War the castle was a Royalist garrison, thought almost
impregnable, and when all other castles had fallen to Parliament save
the nearby Thurland Castle, Royalist fugitives, with their families,
took shelter here. When Colonel Assheton was told to take it he

Hornby Castle

knew only one approach was feasible, that looking to the Wenning
and the east, and there the defenders had their strongest guard.

High "unscaleable precipices" protected the castle on all other
sides, it was said. But someone knew how they could be climbed,
someone who knew Hornby well, and with his guidance the castle
was attacked—from the impregnable and therefore undefended side
—and the Royalists were surprised and overpowered.

Cromwell gave orders after the capture that the castle at Hornby
"be so defaced or demolished that the enemy be prevented from
making any further use thereof".

The eighteenth century saw many changes. The Earl of Cardigan

sold it in 1713 to Colonel Charteris—what a character!—and he
"improved and embellished" in a manner much to the liking of early
tourists, who admired Lord Monteagle's Tower rebuilt "raised up
and fitted in the taste of a modern summer house with sash windows
and gilt frames, a stucco cupola and on top a rich eagle".

Look your fill at the castle from the bridge or the green banks
opposite; that is the nearest you are able to get. It is NOT open to
the public.

More Road Routes

All are on the one inch Ordnance Survey maps, Sheets 95 and 90.

(1) From Slaidburn; a fellroad for those with an eye for fine scenery
and for the wheel at the same time, but definitely *not* for the careless
driver.

From Slaidburn war memorial take the Bentham road north, passing outlying farms above the Stocks reservoir, dropping to Cross o'
Greet over the young Hodder and climbing to the watershed and
skyline. Ahead is the unrolling landscape, like a map across which
goes our road in leaps and bounds; we take the first lane left into
Hindburn dale, through Ivah, Lowgill, to Millhouses and down river
to Wray.

(2) From Wray at Newton's Stores; a peep into Roeburndale "as
far as the road goes" that is, over the breezy open heights at Thornbush, Barkin Gate, over the stripling river and up to the three Salter
farms—for the solitude and the views. Then back again to the fork
roads, left for Hornby and the Lancaster highway.

More Walking Routes

(1) From Slaidburn and Shay Wood; footpaths from farm to farm,
then to the fell gate, along the hard road which tempts motorists
into Croasdale, to the dale head and the old rough track, coinciding
in part with a Roman road, over the solitudes at the county boundary
fence. From the first Salter Fell farm find a path over rough pasture
to Harterbeck, Stauvin, Outhwaite and Wray. A good day's walk!

(2) Again from Hornby or Wray; find the farm of Thornbush at
the foot of Barkin fell around which goes a path, fainter now the
postman no longer walks this part of his round, easily lost in enclosed
dells. Persistence will discover the line of it and from High Barn
the path to Winder farm, high flung on a windy height. The lane
onwards passes over uplands airy before losing height and dropping
into Littledale by the Hall. This is a lovely unsuspected nook, with a
tiny church of St. Ann, a number of quiet farms like seventeenth-

century Cross Gills and a choice of lanes going into the outside world, to Caton or Brookhouse.

(3) From Dunsop Bridge to Wray; a day in or on the fells. Follow the Dunsop River, climb the slopes of Middle Knoll on a rough road or follow Whitendale Beck to the hill-gripped hamlet, aiming for the dale head skyline and the Croasdale road. Here we are on the old track to Hornby given in Route 1.

The "unexploded bomb" notices are rather alarming, but the likelihood of finding one is remote, and no sensible walker would stamp on a peculiar cylinder or suspicious object, deliberately.

Wyre side church, St. Helen's, Churchtown

III The Wyre

WE HAVE ALREADY stood at The Trough Stone in The Trough of Bowland and looked west into Wyresdale realizing its charm.

What an impressive falling away of landscape, and all of it Lancashire! The little stream, its water stained peat-brown, is the infant Marshaw Wyre; it runs out of Featherbed Moss, with merry falls, pools cupped in rocky basins and fringed with ferns, hurrying to the levels of Marshaw. "Just like a highland burn", think many, and the comparison is even more apt down in the conifer woods by Canister House, the lodge of Wyresdale Tower; this is the most popular of picnic spots and bright with family parties on summer days.

All that we look at was part of the royal Forest of Wyresdale; even now the ancient name of Vaccary is given to the townships within the valley, twelve of them which began as small communities where cattle were bred and land farmed on the king's behalf. Marshaw, the first rich green intaken land we pass, was one of them, with Mote Houses where forest laws were administered. Once it had an inn too on the busy Duke's Highway to Lancaster, frequented by pedlars, Scottish traders, packmen and travellers of the poorer sort.

This landscape is the result of careful "improvements" by landowners a century or more ago. A wealthy gentleman, Fenton-Cawthorne, who built Wyresdale Tower in 1806, reclaimed hundreds of unproductive acres, erected a lime kiln at the road verge in The

Trough for the burning of hundreds of tons of lime to be spread on the rushy ground. He enclosed land so limed with miles of stone walls and planted belts of trees by road and river where none had grown before. Later, the Earls of Sefton, the Molyneux who bought the Abbeystead estate, did the same for the lower valley, rebuilding the old farms as well as houses in the village, erecting a great mansion fit to entertain royalty, turning the encircling fells into grouse shoots.

You can persuade farmers to talk of the great shoots, especially of the time when King George V, a fine shot, was guest. Amusing incidents are recalled. One day a young beater—George Drinkall, I think, was his name—got dangerously in the way of the guns.

"Hi, George, look out!" was the shout from all sides. The king it was looked round.

Grouse bark their warnings as we cross the fells. At farms young whelps come leaping boisterously to greet us; they are greyhounds bred on the Sefton farms, future winners of the Waterloo Cup?

Look in through the door of the Game Larder below Marshaw and near the Keeper's House. In Autumn many rows of metal hooks are hung with braces of pheasant and partridge, all destined to be packed in poulterers' vans and sold in towns. Gamekeepers talk of good sport. On the walls are details of a record bag in August 1915 when 2,929 birds fell to the guns on Tarnbrook Fell.

The Vaccaries of Over Wyresdale

Below Marshaw the next vaccary is at Emmott "Ea-mot" where the two rivers meet, and away from the highroad two remote vaccaries, Dunckshaw and Tarnbrook, the latter a nook-shotten spot at the back o' beyond. Where the road dips to a bridge at the vaccary of Lee a road sign points to Tarnbrook, a cul-de-sac, but what a bewitching way it is with the farmyard and complete peace at the end of it. Dead end for cars, this is the beginning of many a fell walk for the energetic; they roam away to Greenside, or up to Wards Stone or White Side, and over to Mallowdale on pathless heights.

A sleepy hollow; children peep round doors, a dog cocks an ear and relapses into a doze, a robin gives a burst of song, someone rattles a milk kit—and silence falls once more.

Four houses complete the number now, one the comely eighteenth-century house built with quiet dignity, where once were "twenty-four smoking chimneys". Its men were makers of felt hats and gloves, and light-footed dancers too. Remember, "Greensleeves" has its old Wyresdale version, the tune being used for a local morris dance by a team of three men, in clogs.

Back to Lower Lee on the highway, once a welcome inn to benighted travellers battered by gales and blizzards on High Cross Moor. Here is a plot of settled calm and behind it acres of green pastures, long ago grazed by royal herds and now by patrician Ayrshires. Against the wall of the great pasture is a long low building on pillars, facing north; this is a Gad House to which, for hundreds of years, cattle stung by the maddening gad fly have raced to shelter, out of the heat of the sun.

The Tarnbrook Wyre flows at the field edge. The path alongside ends at the bridge and Abbeystead village. And here we meet road users who have turned away from the main Trough-Lancaster route.

Abbeystead is full of surprises. It is the last place you expect to see a bus stop, but there it is, with the old pinfold behind it, convenient to lean on, a shelter for the schoolmaster's bee hives, a place to hide away gum boots and wellingtons muddied on the miry paths when you don your town shoes for a jaunt to Lancaster.

The village is full of pretty bits; the post office is in a picture-book cottage and nearby houses bright and shining, embowered in flowers. The school has an ancient foundation from 1674, when "Cawthorne's Endowed School" came into being. The founder, a native, drew up excellent rules; the master had to be of "sound religion, grave behaviour, of sober and honest conversation, no tippler nor haunter of alehouses", and in dealing with the scholars should "season their tender years with good principles in the fear of God".

If you pass the school at playtime or dinner time the youngsters line up on the railings to watch you go by; a fine rosy-cheeked lot they are, knowing nothing but the blessings of good moorland air and country fare.

Another vaccary is not far away at Lentworth; a pocket of Friends have been long established here with a Quaker school and a meeting house in a quiet oasis among the highflung pastures. Across the valley are three others with old names, Haythornthwaite, Swainshead and Catshaw, all farmlands backed by high empurpled fells, with vast windy rough pastures around them and deep cloughs, thickly wooded, going down to the river holms.

Dolphinholm introduces industry, the first sign of it; in 1800 there was a factory here employing a thousand wool spinners and in every house were more, wool combing. Up the steep Waggon Road loads of yarn were carried off to Leeds and Bradford. Dolphinholm's great day used to be the Feast of St. Blaise, patron of wool combers.

What changes since Over Wyresdale was royal forest!

Below Dolphinholm the river enters Nether Wyresdale, wandering through woods to Street Bridge, on near Scorton and out to Garstang, where the great highway from Scotland is carried over its bridges. Farther west it meanders by Churchtown, St. Michael's and many an historic spot, to its estuary and the sea.

Wyresdale Wanderings

BY ROAD

From the Lancashire highroads the natural routes are from Lancaster and Quernmore, or from Clitheroe and Dunsop Bridge through The Trough of Bowland. From Bay Horse or Galgate, on A6, other entries into the upper dale are signposted Abbeystead or Marshaw.

At Marshaw, 3 miles below The Trough boundary stone, the best route crosses the infant Wyre (the watersplash is now replaced by a low bridge) to pass high level and here and there between wild fells and bare pastures. There is little sign of human habitation, but walk away from the road along any of the rough tracks to the right and you come upon old farms on sites of ancient vaccaries near exciting cloughs, like Catshaw Bottoms and Hall Gill. But keep to the road, take the left turns only and you are on Harrisend Fell and the world mapped out below you, from Wyresdale head to the shining estuary of the Lune, over Morecambe Bay to the Westmorland and Cumbrian mountains.

From Harrisend the road enters a region soon to be explored, the valleys of Brock and Calder, and Grizedale.

Take right turns from the Marshaw road and you descend to the Wyre itself, to Dolphinholme and the road to Galgate, or strike minor roads south to Street Bridge, Scorton—a pretty village of gardeners and flower-lovers, a " real picture "—and a gentle countryside across which the river meanders to Garstang.

Below Garstang you cannot avoid the Blackpool-bound traffic going west. Find the village of Churchtown, happily by-passed, with a charming quiet street and a tall market cross on steps, and in the ancient church of St. Helen's—so old some like to think Celtic missionaries founded it on hazardous journeys up the Wyre in frail coracles!—look for the giant timbers from Bowland given by Henry IV for aisle roof, and try to decipher the carved lettering around the south aisle to the effect that " he who talks aloud in church talks only to the devil ".

St. Michael's-on-Wyre has a long history too, and so has the bright little town of Poulton-le-Fylde, not far from the Wyre mouth toll bridge.

BY FOOTPATH

Using the one-inch O.S. Map, Sheet 94, walkers can "read" their way from Marshaw to Abbeystead lake, river edge to Catshaw and emerge at Dolphinholm, battered but unbowed.

Nickey Nook fells from Harrisend

IV Brock, Calder and Grizedale

The Brock

THE BROCK RISES as two infant streams, one from Parlick Foot, the other out of Holme Fell. You might think the next ten miles down to the Fylde plains just a gleesome saunter whereas, in fact, you need stout heart, stouter shoes and a good deal of determination to follow the water edge all the way.

Water-side paths are there, sorely complicated by frequent land slips; to negotiate them sends slippery footsteps sliding—and how the mud sticks! Nevertheless, given a spell of dry weather, soft paths, boggy woodland floors and muddy slides can be circumvented and Brock walking prove quite enchanting.

Bleasdale encompasses great solitude, with acres of rough pasture won from old moorland, where beef cattle are raised—and where Bronze Age natives also hunted and herded their beasts. Bleasdale Circle, one of their burial places and possibly a stockaded village site, is worth tracking down; after which visit the Harris Museum in Preston to see the various antiquities discovered on the spot a century ago.

A circle of valiant farms lies about the rim of this wilderness—Hazelhurst, Fairsnape, Higher Core, Blindhurst, Startifants, Woodyates among them—each with some strips of meadowland and many fell pastures about them. In the middle of the Bleasdale hollow is the little church of St. Eadmor at Admarsh, in an unbelievably green oasis of a churchyard; there is a school nearby and a stony road linking both with the knot of cottages, shop, post office, distinguished by the name of Bleasdale.

Not far below, the Brock begins its wandering through woodlands. This sylvan paradise has a gate by Jack Anderton Bridge; at Gill Barn the two streams become one small, wayward river hiding its whereabouts in larch groves, in beech glades little known by wanderers.

This solitude is for lovers of streams and woodlands, who sense the wonder of it all. They tread softly, knowing they are intruders, that eyes note their passing, squirrels and watching birds report progress and chatter warnings.

With luck you reach Snape Rake dryshod. Here, where the Roman Road from Ribchester to Lancaster tumbles down the wooded bank to the Brock in a water-deepened trough, is a blissful spot worth the overcoming of untold obstacles—pure magic in May when a blue haze fills the scene from water edge to skyline, and deeply moving in Autumn mood.

I often think October and November best become this valley. The sadness of days at the "back end", the mellow light, the blue dusk creeping over deserted places "where man once was and now is not", the reeds turning sere and yellow by half-choked millstreams, and rain of brown leaves falling on silent millponds—all are in harmony.

Pockets of industry once existed in surprising places, up in Bleasdale for instance, at Coolam and Hazelhurst. As over the hills at Tarnbrook, Coolam was a community of felt-hat makers; Hazelhurst once had seventy men and women employed in spinning and weaving, an Inglewhite carrier called Parkington keeping them supplied with combed wool and yarn which he delivered on the backs of three horses. The higher and lower Brock mills were busy then, their wheels turning merrily; at the lower one now sad rows of cottages look over the willow-margined pond, the ruined mill and the overgrown levels of Brock Bottoms. Matshead, local folk will tell you, once made paper and the poor cottagers it employed took "homework" to their families, the making of paper bags.

Brock Villages—Claughton and Inglewhite

The squires of Claughton-with-Brock, the Fitz-Herbert Brockholes, do not take their name from this valley but from Brock Hall near Whalley. Brock, the badger, was already their badge when they came here. The River Brock was long ago known as the "Brook".

Leaving the valley for the main highroad, A6, you cross two bridges, one over the canal, one the railway. When the line was under construction through the Claughton estate the squire of the time insisted on elegant bridges—hence the balustraded Badger Bridge with the brocks in relief on terra-cotta panels.

Claughton is not a clustered village like Inglewhite on the other side of the Brock valley. It straggles along several quiet lanes. Its homes which are almost all farmhouses are trim, well cared for, and the entire landscape wears the settled look of a well-preserved old age, as well it might, for the Brockholes came here many centuries ago and have always cared for the good of the land and the people who worked on it. The Park is vast; within it are pheasantries, coverts for partridge, and if in the evening you watch the direction taken by homing herons, or watch the tentative circling flights of ungainly young birds in Summer, you will locate the Claughton heronry, which in some years had forty or more nesting pairs.

Inglewhite, which is soon reached from a footbridge in Brock Bottoms, is the perfect round-a-green village. It is full of village pride too, being the 1960 winner of the Lancashire best-kept village competition, the neatest, tidiest, and the one which in every way made the most of what it possesses. You would hardly guess it once had a cotton mill and a factory for silk-making, so truly rural is the place today.

Focal point is the pre-Reformation market cross in the middle of the green, on circular steps village children have crawled over and jumped from for over four centuries. Anti-popery zeal destroyed its cross head; the seventeenth century put in its place the little man in costume of the time. Like the best English village it has its inns, and houses round the perimeter of the green which were once inns in the days when far more folk met for the great sheep and cattle fairs.

Both Claughton and Inglewhite have houses which are pleasing from without, but more so within. Some have spice and built-in wall cupboards with eighteenth-century carved doors and butterfly or bat's-wing hinges; one has a handsome oaken staircase round a carved newel post.

At Claughton is a priest's hide over the front door; a peephole in a porch keeps watch on Inglewhite cross. Bedroom floors heave like a stormy sea. Thick timbers arch over inglenooks; forked "elbowed" tree boughs, untrimmed, undisguised, serve for uprights and roof beams. Look for Fleet Street farm north of Claughton and Ashes farm south of Inglewhite—and keep your eyes open wherever you wander by Brock; it is worth while.

The River of Caldervale

One Calder joins the Ribble, another joins the Aire, but neither hides itself so completely as the Calder which finally meets the Wyre. Few ever find it, so enclosed is its valley between high fells near Harrisend and thrusting green hills with fields and hedges to their summits overlooking Caldervale village.

It is full of surprises to a discoverer—a large and expanding paper mill at the dale head at Oakenclough, a busy and cheerful industrial village with two cotton mills in its middle stretch, which looks like a section of a Lancashire town in the coal and cotton belt, taken up bodily and dropped here then forgotten, miles from home.

The brothers Jackson, all Quakers, looked at the valley in 1835 and each found what he required. John chose a site for paper making at Oakenclough, Richard and Johnathan sites for cotton manufacturing downdale, where the Calder provided ample water power and the fells unlimited building stone for factories and a new model village to house the workers.

The brothers had high ideals and strong principles.

There was to be no strong drink, no inn, but here the Jacksons built a temperance hotel with a reading-room. Every house was to have a garden. Annual competitions and shows were arranged to encourage the best use of them.

"An oasis amid the hills", was how Caldervale was described over a century ago, a description which fits today. I like to drop in— literally—from staircase paths which link high-level farms like Landskill and Stirk Hey with Caldervale low level; or down the steep paths from church and schoolyard, where the children leap about like squirrels on their homeward journey. It is very heart-warming to come down from the wind-swept fells to such a cosy, busy, gossipy, friendly place. There are always men not too busy with their gardening to chat awhile; always women talking at doors, enjoying good old chinwags with their neighbours, ready to draw in the passer-by.

And there is always something going on. Caldervale might be cut off from the outside world, but it is very much alive in its own self-contained way. Ask any of the villagers.

They will tell you that days are not long enough, nor the weeks and the months provided with sufficient days to allow them to do all they wish to do.

As in many of the stoniest places I have come across—rocky in their setting, houses of stone, walled-in by stone—the inhabitants are not at all dour or hard. Theirs must be a very good place to live in; so few ever want to leave it, except for the day—for marketing in Garstang or in Preston and Lancaster.

If you have friends and relations who think a factory must be surrounded by untidy squalor and unlovely in its setting, then bring them to Caldervale. The Barnacre Weaving Company mill stands very low by the river, but green fields fill the valley bottom below it. Only a moment away you can be threading the trees in a bluebell wood to emerge on the breezy, grassy pastures of Sollum Hill, with larks carolling, plover screaming, and in spring " cuckoo-cuckoo " is shouted across the land.

A short walk from their front doors and the villagers gaze far away to the Lakeland mountains, the sands of Morecambe Bay and the Lune estuary. There is the tang of the sea in the west wind. Blowing from the east, the wind is full of curlews calling. Once the sound of the horn was loud on Sollum, for this was a preserve of the Tyldesleys of Myrescough Hall. In 1617 King James I was their guest and they gave him good hunting in their Park of Myerscough.

Much of the rich farmland covering the plains to the west is the Queen's estate in the Duchy of Lancaster.

Grizedale

This very unimportant rivulet shares the same fells which see the Calder's beginnings. A short life but a merry one, and the water, impounded in a reservoir, runs below the dam along a most enchanting valley and through charming unsuspected nooks.

Harrisend Fell could not be more bleak and bare, nor the fields around the fell-foot farms more green. Then comes a belt of scented conifers and dark shrubberies, silent but for scuffling blackbirds, and out flows the stream into a hollow drenched in sunshine to fall into a long glittering lake. Nickey Nook is here, beloved by many wanderers—the bracken-clad slopes of Scorton Fell tumbling to the dale on one hand, and wild pathless fells walling it in on the other.

Below the reservoir all is fairy-like, the brook bright between tall birches, hurrying hand in hand with the path towards the wider valley at Throstle Nest. Stream and paths pause, unwilling to leave the song-quivering dale.

ROAD ROUTES AND FOOTPATHS

To discover Grizedale by car leave Garstang for the station east of the town, then turn north and along the lower slopes of Sollum

Hill. Ignore the turns to Caldervale and Oakenclough. Our lane keeps left by the isolated church of Barnacre; soon a narrow way tempts you into the hidden corners of Grizedale, hesitantly, as though it ought not to be there. There are watersplashes and foot-bridges, and Throstle Nest farm, with a welcoming look about it, alone in its secret hollow. Straight on, and a dark and narrow road climbs out—to Scorton.

Walkers may follow riverside paths from Garstang bridge and beyond the disused Knott End railway line, take stiled paths to quiet lanes at Woodacre Hall. Here the route uses a level crossing on the main line. Over the railway an old green track climbs to the hilltop and the same lanes road-users discover.

Near Throstle Nest let the river guide you up and away to the dale head. Out of the plantations Fell End Farm is the first you see, with Harrisend Fell and the high-level road above.

Or, from a point near the reservoir dam climb the bracken-clad breast of Scorton Fell and drop down to the Kennels and the village of Scorton.

Road Routes in the Brock and Calder Country

Use of the one-inch O.S. map, Sheet 94 indicated.
Be prepared to negotiate a veritable labyrinth of bylanes.
I suggest three approaches from the Lancaster-Preston highway.

FROM THE ROEBUCK AT BILSBORROW

The lane is signposted INGLEWHITE. Reaching the village keep on lanes ahead, north to a T-junction, where the road right hugs the edge of Beacon Fell. You may take rough tracks to the fell for heady views above the growing afforestation belt. Or, turning downhill to the left find Hell Clough and the delights of Brock at one of its many bridges, with a cottage smiling at you, a ruined mill near by and quite lovely beech glades to walk through.

Over the bridge the road leaps uphill; left turn back to A6 by way of Claughton-with-Brock; right turn and at attractive route to the upper dale, Bleasdale hamlet and Chipping. Straight forward one lane works roundabout to Sandholme Bridge and the Calder River.

FROM BAMBER'S GARAGE ON A6

Turn right from the highroad, over two bridges; at the T-junction turn right then left for Claughton if you wish to take the byways above Brock to Bleasdale and Chipping.

Turn left at the T-junction through Claughton Park, turning right by a charming seventeenth-century farm at Fleet Street, to carry on to Claughton Smithy and so strike the route sweeping round to the Brock valley. Or, crossing Sandholme Bridge make for Sollum Hill and Caldervale. You may also take the Oakenclough roads from here, to go uphill to Harrisend Fell and the Wyre valley.

FROM BROCKHOLES ARMS, CATERALL

After turning right to Whim Bridge and Fleet Street take the routes given in (2).

Anyone reaching Oakenclough by any of the routes may choose to take the fell road over the Calder Bridge, past the Moorcock inn (opposite which there is a lane to the hilltop church) and descend Delph Lane to the Claughton-Chipping road.

FOUR

HEY FOR THE MOORLANDS

Moorland clough

I Darwen River and the Moors

THE POET DRAYTON wrote of the dirty river which now sidles out of Darwen town towards the outskirts of Blackburn as "the cleere Darwen" and thought it no joke. Mention of Darwen salmon these days—and more than smiles follow.

Ought I to include so sorry a river in this book?

It is not the Darwen's fault that industry has used her so ill. She began well, "as the fair Derwent, river among oak trees". The river still has her moments; her moorland feeders are born high on bold uplands where curlews nest and snipe drum their wings over the uncurling bracken in Spring. Walkers know and love these heights, and many an eye brightens when old folk remember the days they climbed to Darwen Tower with the sun in their faces and as free men walked the ways stalwart defenders of the hill paths had won for them.

From Darwen Tower to the Ribble

You will be told that the Tower on the moor top was erected to celebrate Queen Victoria's Jubilee. That, and something else; a victory won from those who would have closed the old paths by a small band of men who determined their rights should not be taken. Because of them Darwen and Darwenners in the future can take their pleasure up here "for ever".

Centuries ago the valley was considered so fair that many a fine Hall was erected near the flowing river amid scenes of romantic beauty and charm. Hoghton Tower was one, the Hall at Walton, and the two Halls of Livesey and Pleasington, the homes of wealthy Georgian manufacturers at Witton and Feniscowles.

HOGHTON TOWER

The Darwen curves splendidly under the rocky "how" of Hoghton, through woods misted in blue in May, between banks pale rose with buckbean in high summer. On the skyline above the cliffs are the gables and roofs of the Tower—which is, in truth, no tower at all but a splendid Tudor mansion completed four centuries ago. The Tower was blown up when Roundhead forces took over from the subdued Royalist garrison in 1643. Up on the hilltop the walls enclose courtyards alive with memories of historic and royal occasions. In the Great Hall James I did indeed dub the joint of beef put before him, "Sir Loin"—and why not? Hoghton had "done him proud".

On his arrival, household gods of the de Hoghtons in a pageant, had welcomed him—

> "—this house, the heart of all the shire
> Doth bid thee welcome, and would speak it
> In higher notes but extreme joy doth break it",

promising him great sport and pleasure during his stay. The pleasures of the chase ranking big, for the Park was well stocked with deer, the King was able to stand on a mount by the Darwen, still called King's Horr, and bring down the hunted hart where golfers wield the club on Pleasington Golf Course.

LIVESEY HALL AND PLEASINGTON

Lesser families held estates in the valley. The Liveseys were at Livesey in the thirteenth century, and not until 1805 did their manorial lands pass into other hands. Their hall then fell on sad days and now it is but half a house, the wing built in the 1680s is a modern farmhouse whilst the opposite wing with the datestone "1666", is in decay and the Livesey arms have crumbled over the porch leading into the fine dining-hall with its great stone-arched fireplace; birds fly in through the broken windows, and bushes have taken roothold in the huge, built-out chimney.

Across the low-lying fields where the Darwen has made sweeping "S" bends, the Liveseys could once watch the movements of their neighbours, the Ainsworths of Pleasington Hall, a family resident here from the fourteenth century when John de Aynesworth married the heiress of the de Plessingtons who had lived here centuries before that.

Today Livesey Hall stands high with but a few trees as windbreak, whereas Pleasington Hall is in a sheltering arm of wooded hillside and the whole building is charmingly reflected in a pond, with ducks, and daffodils dancing on its banks in March.

BY THE RODDLESWORTH RIVER

Two brothers of the old Blackburn family of Fielden, styling themselves yeomen, chapmen and gentlemen in succeeding generations, moved out of Blackburn at the close of the eighteenth century into estates they had bought in rural solitudes on the Darwen banks, one at Witton where Darwen is joined by the Blakewater, the other at Feniscowles where it receives the Roddlesworth River.

Old Roddlesworth Road near "Rocky Brook"

There, they and their successors tree-planted, landscape gardened, collected about them rare works of art and fine paintings; at Feniscowles, deer were introduced from Scotland and guests were welcomed by their host dressed as a Highland chieftain with Lochaber axe at his side. But both halls have been demolished in recent times, and the doings of the Fieldens are becoming something of a legend.

Countrylovers will find the Roddlesworth most satisfying of the Darwen tributaries. The old halls by this little river have much to show anyone willing to search for "old Lancashire".

Liverpool drowned part of the upper valley, near the Belmont moorland road, planted the slopes reaching up to Darwen Moors, levelled Holinshead Hall, but restored a stone outbuilding as the

"Wishing Well". At higher level many ancient buildings remain, as farmhouses; there is Fine Peters, and the seventeenth-century Higher Hill, Lower Hill—better known as Tockholes Manor House —Crow Trees and Whitehalgh farms, and Red Lees.

On the Darwen Moors

In the wild moors once lived wild men. Around Tockholes tales are still told of secret stills, and excise men in search of the whisky purveyors—I once had the "recipe" from a moor man—and of cockfighting. On Darwen Moors are disused coal pits, with tracks through the heather along which folk used to toil with their ponies —for coal was but sixpence a load at the pit head.

To a stranger this country is bleak, grim, hardbitten; even the names seem harsh to "alien" ears—Tockholes and Winter Hill, Bog Height and Grimehills, Hoddlesden and Pickup Bank, Eccleshill and Blacksnape.

These heights have always nurtured a thrifty, hardworking race of folk, prime example of native hardihood being John Lyon who long ago used his mighty strength to wrestle with the moor top and won a livelihood from his rocky upland acres. Lyon's Den is above Step Back.

The Darwen country was never "easy"; no "soft dimplement" here. Yet those who know it love the surprising solitudes so near streets and factories, in the cloughs gouged out of the moorland slopes, and above all on Darwen Moor where curlews call above the fluttering cotton grass on June days and grouse shoot up screaming from whins and heather, where the sunset sky on July evenings is full of winging swifts and swallows and evening is heralded by the soft whisper of wind in the grasses by Lyon's Den.

Winter has its devotees on the Darwen moors; the Holcombe Harriers have long hunted these heights and there are walkers who come striding along the old tracks though icicles are hanging in the Step Back cascades and Rocky Brook is silent under ice.

> "But oh! for the wild hills that look up at the skies,
> Where the green brackens wave to the wind as it flies!
> Sing hey for the moorlands!

Routes through the Darwen Country

Provide yourself with the O.S. one-inch map, Sheet 95.

The Darwen Tower being so unmistakable a landmark there is really no excuse to lose direction, mists being absent.

FROM THE ROMAN ROAD

Road users from Bolton pass through Turton and Edgworth to hit the Roman way near Wayoh, this road being the ancient highway to Blackburn before the new low-level route was made through Darwen town. There are most impressive bird's-eye views over the town, a sprawling mass of bricks and mortar, slate and native stone, spiked with tall chimneys, and the high moor about it.

In a dip of the road, by the Crown and Thistle inn at Whittlestone Head, a place where you can picture waggoners and horses, pack-horses and packmen straining and toiling over earlier stone-paved ways, there is plenty of atmosphere. Even more can be felt on straying down the track to old farms like Jackamans and lonely spots on the heathery moors beyond the Sough Tunnel, over wild wastes to Bull Hill.

FROM BELMONT MOORS

A road going towards Darwen Moor edge leads above the plantations of Holinshead Hall to Tockholes. From this can be found the stony road down to Rocky Brook, or a climbing path to the moor top at Lyon's Den and so to the Tower.

From the Royal Hotel, Tockholes—a track makes direct over rough pastures to the Step Back, a deep defile in the moors, with the Tower reached from its upper edge. "Step back. Go no farther!" said Cromwell. (?)

From the Victoria, Tockholes—go downhill to find the Manor House and Crow Trees, both ancient houses, wander off to find the Chapel, a cradle of early nonconformity, and the parish church.

From the Rock Inn, Tockholes—Rock Lane also makes for the church, which has an open-air pulpit in the tiny "National" school wall, the Toches stone at its door and a history going back to the seventh century.

From the Hare and Hounds at Abbey village—tread the fieldpath to a many-stepped stairway into Engine Bottoms—signs of old industry, memories of secret whisky stills—and climb up to Red Lees, seventeenth century and "haunted" they say! You may walk on to the Manor House and Tockholes.

Path to Rivington Pike above Tigers Clough

II Rivington Pike, Yarrow and Douglas Rivers

The Pike and Winter Hill

RIVINGTON HAS BEEN known by many names in its time. It was Roving—the rough hill—it was Roynton or Ryven Pike when Winter Hill was Winterhold Pike or Winterheld.

I like the name Winterheld, for winter does indeed grip tight upon the moors where Yarrow and Douglas spring, ice skims the pools and snow lies unmelted in gullies when walkers in the low lands are thinking of April and daffodils.

Fairlokke, another name, was well earned. A fair prospect there is from the Pike. As Roby wrote, "The view from this elevated spot should the day be favourable certainly repays the adventurous— but not infrequently an envious mist or passing shower will render these efforts unavailing to scan the wide creation."

A pity we cannot shelter inside the Tower as was originally

intended when, in 1732, Mr. Andrews of the Hall at the hill foot erected it "for the convenience of rest and shelter for those whom curiosity urges to the fatigue and peril of the ascent".

I wonder what the perils were to the climber two centuries ago? They are lacking now. Why, the last time we were on the Pike, a young man asked if we would care for a lift back to Belmont; his car was just below. He was one of those pioneering types who enjoys seeing how much punishment his car will take before packing up.

Mr. Andrews' tower occupies an ancient beacon site. In the fateful waiting days of 1588 Salford Hundred paid out sixteen pence a day to men "for watching the Becon". And the Armada never came!

Now around Bolton are many keen and energetic amateur archaeologists who believe prehistoric hillmen knew the Pike site and hunted the heights of Rivington and Anglezarke.

Local names are food for thought—Round Loaf, Standing Stone Hill, Devil's Dike, Noon Hill and Two Lads—but the archaeologists do more than think. They range the hilltops, bog and mire, rocky knoll and boulder spill, with maps and hammer. A stone-edged dip, a raised dike, and stony patch made clear after moor fires, a slight rise of land on windy skylines—each is examined by seeing eyes.

A coin, a bead, a scrap of flint or chert with signs of man's work upon it, each find helps to build up a picture of the remote past when men lived and buried their dead near the headsprings of Douglas and Yarrow.

A wet summer a few years ago saw a party at work on Noon Hill; they excavated a Bronze Age burial mound, with urns and tools as their finds. They look at Two Lads, that nobbly hilltop not far from Scotsman's Stump, and wonder what might have been unearthed there if men had not upset the site by so much earlier piling of stones.

Two Lads has its legends. Long ago, tales tell, two cairns were piled over the resting place of two shepherd lads bewildered by storm, who perished here. Or the stones mark the graves of two young Pilkingtons, or two princes of Anglo-Saxon times; take your choice.

There were two cairns on the hilltop in former times—most likely prehistoric. A century or so ago men raised a round platform of dressed stone and piled the Two Lads' cairn we see today, maybe borrowing stones from the original cairns, destroying at the same time valuable evidence.

Do you regret the modern, sky-reaching landmarks now on Winter Hill; the police radio control pylons and the soaring ITA mast? Many do, remembering the remote, far from the world feeling which belonged to the moorland tracks but a few years ago.

LC   M

To recapture the old feeling of isolation just take the path, or the new road, to Scotsman's Stump on a day when all is shrouded in mist and though you cannot see the mast as you draw near you can hear the roaring of gales as they come in contact with the steel framework, a frightening sound like the engines of heavy bombers bearing down.

On such a day, clouds low over Winter Hill and Belmont Moor, an old man called in passing, " A grand day for a murder ! "

An odd remark to pass to strangers on a lonely road we thought. But it was November 9th—anniversary of the day when George Henderson, traveller of Annan, a young man of nineteen was " brutally murdered on Rivington Moor ".

This is told on the memorial called Scotsman's Stump—near the foot of the mast, hard by the source of the River Douglas.

On that foggy November day in 1838 many trudged the hill tracks to the coal pits. Henderson and his companion were familiar to most of them and their movements, their accustomed way from Belmont to Blundell Arms and Moorgate, well known. Out of the murk several heard a cry, " I'm robbed ! I'm killed ! ", and rushing to the spot found the dying man. Though the fog prevented their evidence being accepted by the judge at the trial many were convinced they could identify the men who had been seen lurking on the moors before the murder, waiting to waylay the two pedlars. One they believed guilty was killed soon afterwards in a roof fall in the pit—retribution had followed swift !

Local folk will tell you, " For years, on the anniversary of the murder, a Henderson came from Scotland to play a lament on the bagpipes at Scotsman's Stump ".

An old man once said, " I could tell of things as happened on these moors would mek your hair curl." He doubtless referred to the days of illicit whisky distilling and excise men giving chase to those who thought to evade the law. It was too simple to distil whisky, if you knew how. Cock fighting too was a local outdoor sport.

Below the Pike is a No-Man's-Land, a Secret Garden world, a Sleeping Palace wilderness full of sad memories and whispers of happier days. At the beginning of the century that " lad from Bolton ", who became the wealthy soap magnate, Lord Leverhulme, visualized a sort of Italian villa above terraced gardens as his moor-edge home. Money no object; his Bungalow was built, expert gardeners designed on a grand scale, earmarking rocks from the hillside to create waterfalls and grottoes, collecting rare shrubs and plants from the four corners of the world, to make the hanging gardens of Rivington bloom like the rose.

We often wander and lose ourselves in the same gardens now for they have for many years returned to nature. Roynton Cottage is levelled, the Lodges too; car owners have come by subterfuge to slice off the turf of shaven lawns for their own gardens; boots of cars have rocked down Georges Lane full of uprooted plants and loads of evergreen; little boys play at scouts under broken-down loggias and, in rainy weather, inside oriental and Italianate summer-houses. We have crept down leaf-levelled stone staircases from terraced gardens to ornamental lakes, and picnicked by still pools fed by waterfalls coaxed into them from moor-edge springs, and pushed aside the interwoven branches of rhodos and azaleas barring lost paths. But breaking through there have been sensational rewards. There is a theatrical effect about the stone balconies and the views opening out from them. There should be cobalt blue lakes and cypress groves below, ruinated temples and suntanned peasants carrying loads of grapes. Instead—the softer water-colour washes of a Lancashire landscape, lakes reflecting more delicate blue skies, and muted green and grey distances.

Lever Park was another gift to Rivington; some remember the game reserves, fenced-in compounds, where children watched giraffe, zebras, kangaroos, deer and ostriches, goggle-eyed. And once a sacred cow!

The lakes of Rivington and Anglezarke attract streams of motorists and many walkers here on Summer days. Liverpool is responsible for the lakeland landscape which has in the last century taken the place of green valleys and scattered farms; apart from the two embankments and the masonry at the lower end of each lake the verge is not un-beautiful, thanks to Nature's kindly mantling. Often we almost forget the lakes are man-made. From the Pike they look almost natural.

Seen from the Horwich-Chorley road, with a misty day blurring the landscape, the stretch of water, the ruins of the castle above the shore (erected by master masons from plans of the castle of the Molyneux, which once stood where Queen Victoria surveys the heart of Liverpool), and the wooded hillside rising to the Pike "make a picture"; distance lends pure enchantment to this view.

Beyond the lakes the marks of industry are heavy. The Douglas River wanders over the mosses below the ridge of Blackrod—a region where you can see peat cutting and turf stacked as on the bogs of Ireland—then on through towns, and villages which can hardly be distinguished from the towns, to Wigan. The Yarrow, after passing through the lakes, running through the little valley by Roaring Lion and Abyssinia to Limbrick and Cowling, passes near the town of Chorley.

Headless cross

We trace their diverse courses from the Pike. We lose them for a while in the maze of towns and confusion of urban and industrial development. Above the smudge of smoking chimneys rise the long green hills sloping away gently west of Standish and Wigan. Beyond them the two rivers meet again, in the lowlands of Lancashire.

Then comes the seaboard, and a flash of silver tells us that the tide is flowing towards the promenades of Southport, St. Annes, Blackpool. We count the ships sailing, the liners steaming out of the Mersey—riding in the sky it seems. We watch boats approaching the Ribble estuary. Liverpool Bay is south-west—then south of it the long, low, blue-grey wave of the mountains of North Wales. The Ribble mouth and the Fylde too are clear—and far away the hint of blue-grey which is Lakeland, the mountain ranges of Furness and Cumberland.

For map readers; the country about the Yarrow and Douglas comes across the corners of four O.S. one-inch maps—Sheets 94 and 100, the high moors on 95 and 101.

Rivington Village

"About Lidcote Moss under a hille is Riven or Riventon on a water called Anderton Ford which joins the Yarrow."

That was the village below the Pike as described four centuries ago when the Pilkingtons were still lords of the manor and lived in the Hall of their ancestors. What they looked like can be seen from the copy of an old painted mural. in the nave of the church, less clearly from the dark original at the Grammar School. Richard Pilkington, Bishop of Durham, is portrayed in Tudor dress with his six sons kneeling behind him and his wife facing him heading a line of praying daughters. One Pilkington rebuilt the church, another founded the grammar school.

The rules he made are strict, to our way of thinking. School began at six in the morning. The boys were encouraged to play manly sports, but forbidden to indulge in dicing, gaming, bowls, haunting alehouses, to take part in brawls or to carry any weapon but penknives into class. Many boys were lodged in local houses; at night they were told to read a passage from the scriptures to the assembled family.

There is a new grammar school now; the old site has a primary school. Later owners rebuilt the Pilkingtons' hall—in 1694, and again in 1774—but the massive barns they left—one called Hall Barn, the other Great House Barn—both so skilfully restored by Lord Lever-hulme's craftsmen they look like weathering another thousand years. For some believe the huge beams and crucks were of local oak felled before William came to conquer.

I wonder what the ghosts of returning Pilkingtons would say on being spectators of the Saturday night Hall Barn dances—very lively "do's" with coaches bringing young folk from far and near?

Few farms are left of the many mentioned on old maps of Riving-ton. They took their owners' names—Old Kate's, Parson Bullough's, Derbyshire's. One was Moses Cocker's, a character remembered as an early inventor of a "flying machine" which he was anxious to try out from Mr. Andrew's new tower on the Pike. Fortunately, he was advised instead to take off from the barn roof of his own farmyard; his landing was soft—in the midden!

If you hear one bell ringing some Sunday afternoon, track down the sound to the Unitarian chapel, that interesting little building dated 1703, at the foot of the road from Belmont. Before the days of toleration, local dissenters worshipped in a secret place below Noon Hill. This was the chapel they built when licences were granted. It has high calf-box pews, a fine pulpit and the lengthy memorial to

Lord Willoughby of Parham, one of the wealthy family benefactors to
early dissenters in this district.

Healey Nab

Every Lancashire town has one nearby hill it claims as its own. No
doubt about Chorley's—Healey Nab to the east of it, reached by
tracks climbing through copses of oak and birch, from Bagganley,
Crosse Hall or Healey. Old ways they all are, especially those
defined by massive boulder-piled walls which climb to hilltop pastures.

Two contrasting regions are viewed from the top. Westwards is the

Anglezarke Lake and Rivington Pike from Healey Nab

town and blurr of smoke; east, the fields and farms of White Coppice
the stark moors stretching away to Great Hill, Anglezarke and Belmont; and southwards, a heavenly sight on a blue June day, the long
lakes and the hillsides above the Yarrow.

Most streams called " Black " are old boundaries. There is a Black
Brook down below, falling from a deep clough in Great Hill, an
ancient division between " Gunolfes Moores " and Healey Park. In
the thirteenth century the countryside hereabouts was in the Park
of Leyland, a royal forest, the hill on which we stand was imparked
and its revenues from agistment, the wintering and summering of
many cattle, from pannage—beech mast and acorns were feed for

swine—was due to the king. Wild cattle grazed its enclosures; you may look for the earthen banks and broken walls which are all that remain.

The Park was so well stocked and offered such good loot that in 1322 Scots raiders thought it worth risk to make inroads as far south as this. They swept over the Ribble, headed for Healey and drove away many beasts. That year the king received no revenue for cattle gisted or swine fattened on the Nab.

Healey Park was worth having; leaseholders were at times Standishes of Duxbury, Barrets, Hollands and Lovells. When Edmund Crouchback became Duke of Lancaster he gave it to a Garnett, one of a family long important in the organization of the royal forests in Lancashire, and from them it passed to the Dacres.

Old names around the Nab; Blake broke, the Pales of Healey Cliffs, the Haia of Healey. When forest land was cleared for cultivation the name "leah" came on the map, as in Bagganley, Knowley, Astley.

You want to climb the Nab? Then take your choice from the paths visible from the Chorley side, or from Anglezarke lake and the Waterman's House at the lake head scramble up the path which rises steeply over a wall and through a wood. Soon, at the modest height of 682 feet you will feel "monarch of all you survey".

The Yarrow River

From the top of the moorland road which crosses from Belmont to Rivington you look down Hordern Clough and the beginning of the Yarrow. The Celtic name "Garw", the rough and stormy water, fits it well; just here it is very much like the Yarrow river of ballad and song as it runs down to its "dowie holms". A pity no ballad singers ever extolled our river or told its tales of romance and tragedy.

The subject matter was there. Take the abduction of Margery, Ralph Pilkington's lady—the coming of a band of wife-stealers to Rivington; maybe the lady was willing for she was up and off with them, and even the order of the king to the High Sherif did not restore her to the husband. Then there was the stormy interlude involving men of Rivington and Heath Charnock, all most anxious to be guardians to the five orphaned daughters—the youngest in the cradle and the eldest thirteen—of Street of The Street; they came " in riotous manner arrayed as for war " and threatened to burn down the house if their uncle did not give them up.

Anglezarke a thousand years ago was a community of Anglian farmers grazing their kine by Yarrow water. Half the meadows and pastures of the old community are drowned under the reservoirs.

The Yarrow too merges with other streams, until out it creeps, flows through " Abyssinia ", round the borders of Heath Charnock, washing the walls of Limbrick, Cowling, and through the woods of Duxbury where once stood the Hall of the Standishes.

Too often we come upon " site of " on Yarrow banks. The Duxbury Standishes lived for generations in valley and woodlands; a son sailed to America in the *Mayflower* and helped to put the new colony on a firm footing; he was Miles Standish. The Gillibrands have gone too, and the family of Park Hall—but Astley Hall remains, safe in the care of Chorley's town fathers.

A Park is next best thing when the country is too far away, think the townsfolk of Chorley promenading the long drive and roaming the paths of the rivulet at Astley Hall. The loveliest surprise as we emerge from the paths or drive is the sight of the Hall, its splendid seventeenth-century façade reflected in the ornamental lake; when the evening sun winks in its windows it glows like a casket of jewels. Which is what it is; inside are many treasures, Tudor carvings, ornate plaster ceilings and a superb shovelboard table in the Long Gallery, among them.

Many old farmsteads have been swept away from the valley between Chorley and Euxton. Fortunately the latter has kept its church with a Norman doorway, heavily buttressed walls and a steep-pitched west-end gable overlooking the busy highroad. It possesses a pulpit too which came into the news in January 1854, when astonished parishioners read how " apparatus for whisky distillation has been found by a joiner under the pulpit of Euxton church ", and with growing concern heard of the coming of the Excise Officer from Chorley, his obtaining a search warrant from Captain Anderton of the Hall, a J.P. so that he could enter church—and parsonage ! Later they breathed sighs of relief when the incriminating evidence proved not the Rev. Mr. Williams guilty, but the Sexton, who had disposed of the still in the pantry, the worm in the coach house and the rest in the vestry. He had been able to make six gallons of whisky a night !

Some pretty bits of gentle landscape follow, from Pincock Bridge and the old mill down to the quiet pastures of Eccleston. The church with its pinnacled and turreted tower—four weather cocks tell the way the wind blows—the tall trees around the churchyard, the old corn mill whose wheel was driven by the Yarrow, the arched red sandstone bridge, all are component parts of the happiest picture of rural England. Closer investigation is equally rewarding. Just as in Chorley church where we find links in pews and memorials with the Standishes, the Charnocks, Crosses, Parkers and Gillibrands who owned the land by Yarrow and dwelt in great halls—here at Eccleston are memories of landowning families whose histories affected this countryside—the Dicconsons of Wrightington, the Crispes of Parbold, the Hawksheads of Heskin, the Rigbys of Harrock Hall.

Between banks of green willow, with cornfields on either hand, the Yarrow slows down, meandering lazily towards Croston. First through the Park of the Hall, the present house reminiscent of a French château, red brick walls and stone quoins and facings. Next it flows under the corn mill bridge at the end of Grape Lane and under the boughs of great beeches towards that most rectorial of rectories in which Rawsthornes have lived through many generations. It is half a house now, but the most satisfying façade remains; the seventeenth-century gables are masked by a new eighteenth-century curved roofline.

The Rectory fields were formerly scene for the final jollifications following the Croston Wakes. Ask old folk and they will recall dancing to bands, fireworks—and once a balloon was launched. What an innocent face the Yarrow has flowing between the cottages of Croston! Who could believe tales of the destruction caused by its risen waters in past years, the bursting of banks, flooding of the graveyard, filling up of graves, seeping into the church nave, undermining its foundations, and a toll of deaths by drowning?

The land around is low-lying. Folk travelling to the Mother Church frequently encountered floods impassable; therefore one by one, with Chorley leading the way, the outlying districts of Hoole, Rufford, Bretherton, Hesketh-with-Beckonsall, Mawdesley and Bispham pleaded for the formation of daughter parishes with churches of their own.

History began long ago in these parts with the coming of St. Aidan to the river side settlements, early in the seventh century, and the founding of a cross-town. There is no other Croston in the United Kingdom, the post office assures me. The tall cross on its steps looked up Church Street to St. Michael and all Angels; centuries ago the shaft was broken and Croston had no cross, only a village pump against the steps and socket stone. Recently it was decided high time to replace the cross so, from a large millstone found in the neighbouring smithy, one was cut and again Croston lives up to its name.

Because of its dedication, Michaelmas was always a local time of festivity; now Croston Wakes are held at Old Michaelmas which comes early in October and what a day it is, though shorn of much of the exuberance which made some think it was not quite respectable to show interest in it.

" Church Street," said an octogenarian who was born there, " hasn't changed a bit ". It is the best example of an eighteenth-century street, cobbles and all, you can expect to find anywhere. Look at the dates on the walls, and look at the houses from across the river.

The Yarrow sidles under the garden walls. Once when the waters were in flood and high against the back doors, daredevil lads would take headers from the kitchen doorsteps into the river and take a dip. Some were swept away.

Between the churchyard and the water is the school on the site of the one founded in 1283 when the Priest was granted a licence by John of Gaunt. Small children were carried away from the play-

Church Street, Croston

ground railings by the river in spate. How mothers feared Yarrow in flood!

A young boy leaning on the Town Bridge was tossed into the Yarrow by a bull being led to Croston Fair and his body found far downstream.

Only a few miles below Croston the Yarrow is joined by the diminutive Lostock river and flows to meet the Douglas at Red Bridge.

The two rivers now pass through the land of morass and swamp, once a wild and lawless country dominated by turbulent families like the Banastres of Bank. Few strangers ever penetrated into the moss land "Inter Ripam and Mersham". They called it Christ's Croft, a no man's land, secure retreat for wanted men, home of lost causes.

> "When all England is aloft
> Safe are they that are in Christe's Croft.
> And where should Christe's Crofte be
> But between the Ribble and Mersey?"

The Banastres looked to the mossland for security whereas their successors at Bank Hall, the Fleetwoods of the seventeeth and eighteenth century, tried to reclaim the marshes, to make them not the enemy of man with their Will o' the Wisps and Jack o' Lantern, their marsh fevers and agues, but good farming land. Others were to succeed where they failed, making the flat country between the Douglas and the sea a vast market garden, divided into geometrical fields, drained by long straight dykes, crossed by ruler-straight roads. The river and the canal, the Douglas Navigation, were full of boats bringing coal and slates from North Wales, lime and limestone from north Lancashire, transporting the produce of the lowland farms, the coals from Wigan, bricks from Tarleton, stone from the Parbold quarries, to other parts of the north-western coast where there was a demand for them.

A century ago this was still windmill land; the corn mill at Bretherton is now a modern residence. The river was still busy with boats—as it had been from Tudor days when the Stones owned sea-going craft and imported from Ireland cargoes of oak timber for the use of hall-building families like the Shuttleworths of Gawthorpe.

You can see the house the three Stones brothers built so proudly in 1613, south of Hoole—near the old Bretherton toll house; but how sad it is, "garrulous of better days", its fate uncertain, cracks in the brick walls, and tall chimneys atilt!

It laments better times, and one particular day Carr House remembers—a November afternoon in 1639 when the lodger in the porch chamber, Jeremiah Horrocks, the young Hoole curate, recorded through its window the Transit of Venus. This did put Carr House and Hoole on the map, and into books on astronomy and astral sciences.

Sad winds wail over the level landscape between Hoole, Hesketh and Beckonsall as the river makes its way to the Ribble and the sea.

The Douglas River

The Douglas, "'the dark river" in the Celtic tongue, the "creeping Duglesse" of Camden, the "swart Dulas" of Michael Drayton—

and a river so many pity today, poor thing, wandering unhappily through such miserable, smoke-begrimed, dismal, drab country. Lancashire, we know, has regions where man has made a mess of the countryside. But the Douglas has her moments—a good beginning and a pleasant ending.

I remember a Midsummer morning, dragging ourselves out of bed at 2.30 to climb from the Chorley Old Road at the Jolly Crofters, above Wallsuches and Montcliffe to watch day break on Winter Hill by the Douglas springs. We saw and heard day being welcomed by a rising of larks, the morning calling of curlews, cuckoos, and the early alarums of red grouse. The sun turned the wilderness of rushes, whins and bent grass to red gold; it gilded the ear tips of a hare as it stopped in its course amazed to see such early intruders in its own domain—in that magic moment when it tipped over the moortop, a fiery red disc.

It is most impressive to look on Lancashire lying asleep, wrapped in cotton-woolly blanket of morning mist, and in the crisp clear air to hear the first sounds of awakening—a distant hooter, the first train whistle from Horwich. Then wisps of smoke rise from factory chimneys. The sleeping world is waking, stirring, about to go about its daily business.

The Douglas from its springs drops from the moors into deep cloughs between bracken-clad banks, many cloughs each taking in one of its feeders. One is Tigers Clough, one dark ravine in the hillside where it is not so impossible to imagine that Horwich was forest land once, within the Barony of Manchester and with three sworn foresters of its own demanding bread, drink and victuals from the tenants. There are tales of a sort of tavern of those days. Was it Tiger's in the Clough?

The foresters ranged these hills. They held forty two oxgangs of land hereabouts. In Spring they summoned the hale and hearty men of Horwich to go forth into the ravines and seek out trees wherein hawks were nesting. Six centuries ago no region was better breeding ground than this and the King's mews needed constant replenishing. They reported back to the foresters who from that time until St. Barnaby—June 11th—kept day and night watch on the nests. So valuable were the birds when hawking and falconry were royal sports. The whole community saw to the foresters' needs whilst the watch was on. Then—the eggs hatching out—the villagers had another outdoor expedition, this time to climb to the nests and remove the hawks' chicks, delivering them to the foresters or the king's bailiff.

If any man in Horwich said he was otherwise engaged he had to receive his punishment, which took the form of ploughing half an acre of cleared forest land near Manchester; he received some token payment for his labours—one penny! I think most chose the bird-nesting.

Not far from the young river, on tributary streams, we come across old farms with walls so thick they appear to be pushing themselves back into the earth. Look for Ormestones, the Manor House, and in the hollow behind Horwich church the ancient homesteads of Wilderswood, Foxholes, Mill Hole and Crowthers Fold. There are tales here of a Crompton's experimental "Mules", of an early factory and child labour.

The best tales of old Horwich we hear from folk who once worked at Wallsuches.

Everyone who travels Chorley Old Road in spring goes on his way with his heart "dancing with the daffodils" of Ridgmont Park. Ridgmont was a Regency mansion built by the Ridgways, bleachers of Wallsuches, about which so many stories can be gathered. The most picturesque, of doubtful authenticity, tells how two Ridgway brothers left Bolton pushing a cart into the country. Somewhere about the Blundell Arms a wheel came loose and ran away downhill. The two brothers gave chase. "Where it stops," they said, "we'll build the works which is to make our fortunes."

The wheel trundled down a rough lane and came to rest in a dip at the moor foot. There the Ridgways built a bleachworks, a collection of many buildings all needed for the various processes involved.

The many springs of good clear water on Makinson Moor filled a number of lodges. A new straight road brought down stone from the hillside quarries to the site.

Among the tall buildings was the truck shop where on pay day several assistants were ready to do trade with the workpeople. There were large four-pound loaves freshly baked, best shin beef at fourpence a pound, and a great quantity of wholesome and good quality foodstuffs at reasonable prices.

There is something fascinating about the echoing cobbled yards of deserted works like Wallsuches. Wander some day down the rough lane opposite the Jolly Crofters in Upper Horwich—the way of the runaway wheel?—and look over the lower lodge to the sunny green pastures where finest beef cattle once grazed near the "tenter grounds". No one stirs at the bleachworks, but the Shambles where the meat was slaughtered—the Bakehouse where the crusty loaves were baked, and the Truck Shop, you can find them and ruminate, if you will, on factory days "then and now".

I know an old man of ninety-six. He began work at Wallsuches as a half-timer—eight years old—yet how eagerly his mother took his weekly wages, fourpence a day, into the family purse. One week the child employees worked the 6 a.m. to noon shift and to Horwich school in the afternoons; the alternate weeks it was school in the morning and work from noon to 6 p.m. His first job was singeing cloth in the dye house. As a young man he remembers bringing home sixpence at the end of the week—a period of short-time work—and that was all left after rent and grocery had been deducted.

The lodges near Wallsuches are reverting to nature. We stand quite still to watch the progress of a weasel, leaping in graceful curves by the half-dried mill stream. Magpies chatter, blackbirds sing their loudest on the trees overhanging Th'Urn—the clear spring to which a lad was sent with jugs to quench the bleachers' thirsts on hot days —long ago.

It seems odd to see stacks of dark turves on the old mossland below Horwich and Blackrod where the Douglas takes its way. Peat was everyone's fuel in the past, in spite of the nearness of many coal pits.

The pristine freshness of the valley has gone. There are a few pretty spots where the children of Adlington and Blackrod play—like the secluded dells of Aberdeen—and at Arley Hall, within its still moat and girdle of tall trees, poignant memories of a past when all was fresh and fair, and everything the eye looked at was pleasant.

Above the valley rise the breezy heights of Aspull Moor, the windy hills of Haigh—with a windmill in midfield—and long tree-clad ridges hiding Wigan. But remember, much around Wigan is far less black than it is painted!

Take Haigh Hall and the Plantations, not quite country, but, says a Wigan Jane, "a rollicking ride behind the tractor trailer for me"— long miles of gloomy avenues, a river in a red-rocky bed and at the end—the charm of old gardens, lilies opening in sunken pools. I cannot hope to persuade countrygoers to make a special journey for the purpose of tasting the pleasures of Haigh and its plantations for themselves, but for anyone passing by!

At school we all learnt about the early canal engineers of the eighteenth century. At Haigh the Bradshaighs had the idea of carrying surplus water from their mines of cannel coal in a Great Sough, three centuries ago, this leading to further canalizing attempts which became the first waterways. The Great Sough you may look down on from the drives, excavated through the red rock.

One story of Haigh is worth repeating. In 1842, a year of great disturbance, with riots among the workers of Lancashire, certain Wigan miners planned to attack the Hall by night. The Haigh miners were officially on strike too. But would they allow the Old Lord to be disturbed? Not they. They made a cordon round the house for, said they, "We'll see Old Lord (Crawford) has his port in peace."

Nothing put the villages of the Douglas valley so firmly on the eighteenth-century map as the canalizing of the river. Cheap transport caught up the trade of Hoole, Tarleton, Rufford, Parbold and Appleby Bridge, and how they prospered!

Between Yarrow and Douglas

Anyone expecting to find the grime of town and coalmine disfiguring miles of landscape between the two rivers must be pleasantly surprised to find such charming rurality. Cornfields sweep over rounded hills, snug old farmhouses are scattered about and houses once "stately homes of England" still stand in ornamental grounds which were the pride of their owners two and three centuries ago. There is no need to feel apologetic when bringing friends to look at this Lancashire. Watch their faces when confronted by Wrightington fish ponds in the glory of flowering azalea and rhododendrons, at the brighter than pure gold of Ashhurst Hill when gorse is in bloom, at the breezy slopes of High Moor, and their amazement at the tremendous panoramas spread around.

Local names are a fascinating collection. Mab's Cross (with Wigan's favourite legend woven around it), Skull House Lane, Hunger Hill, Cat in t' Window, Dangerous Corner, Hell Hob—each has its tale.

Arthurian legend has links with Martin Mere and with the battlefield near Ince and the Douglas. Does this surprise strangers, that Lancashire the hard-headed and forthright should treasure such local lore?

Wait till they are taken to Mawdesley.

Mawdesley, hidden away between Harrock Hill and the mosslands, has a House of the Skull at Lane End; they say it is the skull of George Haydock, a young priest martyred in 1583, a sad relic in a glass casket up in an attic once used as chapel by local Roman Catholics. There is also a Skull House Lane some miles away, near the Douglas at Appley Bridge.

Mawdesley, repository of old tales if ever there was one, has an inn, the Black Bull, which no one locally ever calls anything but Hell Hob. In the cosy bar parlour, clamped to the side of a fireplace, is a giant of a poker, sixteen pounds in weight, the lifting of which "to poke the fire of Hell Hob", was the cause of many wagers lost and won in the old days when the inn was Hell in Mawdesley. The landlord, for the attraction of more customers, once exhibited a bottle containing an imprisoned spirit, that of a ghost who had wandered wailfully around Hall and inn. When the credulous feared the bottle might break and the "influence" wander abroad once more, fears were allayed by a ceremonial throwing of the bottle into a pit. Where doubtless it still lies!

One wandering way from Mawdesley to Wigan is by the Dangerous Corner at Wrightington; where a hearse on the way to a burial jolted as the horses stumbled and up sat the dear departed; a funeral breakfast was turned into a joyful homecoming. But some time later the good wife died "again" and was taken off for a second funeral. This time the husband sat by the driver of the hearse. Coming up to the scene of the previous extraordinary resurrection he was heard to whisper—"Now then—take good care—this is a *very* dangerous corner!"

What of Hunger Hill nearing Standish? Did Cromwellian soldiers feel a-hungered here?

And Cat i' t' Window? I have three local derivations for the name. The house near Pepper Lane, some say, was used for the celebrations of Mass in the penal days, and a figure of a cat on the sill told Roman Catholics that a priest would be there that night.

The Standish family were known for their Stuart and Jacobite sympathies. One hid from enemies in the house; a cat dozing peacefully in the sun on the window seat allayed the suspicions of men sent to seek him. Why search? If a stranger was within the feline would look less relaxed.

Was he the same Standish implicated in the plotting in James II time who sought the aid of a dairy maid to hide him from pursuers? He just missed detection when a sword blade came within an inch of his skin as he crouched beneath bedding in a chest.

Upholland across the Douglas valley has its share of equally colourful traditions. Behind the church and Priory founded by "good Sir Robert Holland" once stood a great hall wherein all the poor of the neighbourhood were given hospitality; they flocked to the table and those left outside for lack of room on feast days filled their sacks with doles of food. Sir Robert, in the difficult days of Edward II, joined Thomas, Earl of Lancaster, in rebellion against the King. Their cause lost, he became an exile, a barefoot wanderer begging alms in the towns of Flanders.

Ask anyone in Upholland about the Robber's Grave at the top end of the hillside graveyard.

George Lyons was in the tradition of Robin Hood, robbing the rich to give to the poor. They caught him stealing new-baked bread from the Owl Inn—for which crime he was hanged high on the gallows.

An exciting hill road leaves the village, making for the heights of Ashhurst—and what a spot to be on a clear, windy day! The beacon—called The Beetle—was erected in 1798 when daily warning of a French invasion was expected. Men stood ready on night and day ward. But no French came.

By the way, you do not need to believe that you can see every one of the sixteen counties promised from the Beacon. I have counted —maybe ten—with the naked eye, but no more.

Three centuries ago a local diarist, Roger Lowe, visiting friends, the Scotts at Ashhurst, wrote, " As we were going we looked up and down, stood upon a hill and saw the land round about. It is the pleasantest place that ever I saw, a most gallant prospect." He added —" we got wimberry ".

Parbold Bottle is good for equally gallant prospects—Billinge Hill too, with its Stump and tales of Cromwell's long shot to the tower of Upholland church, and every high point on the hills facing west, across the plains to the sea.

Down below; canal country, old windmills, their strength taken, corn mills and cornfields, charming unspoilt villages like New-burgh, and Lathom Hall once " a little town in itself, the glory of the county " and so handsome a residence that Henry VII took ideas for his new palace at Hampton when guest there. The demolitions after the long siege in 1644, when Lady Derby held out so valiantly against Cromwellian forces, ended the glory that was Lathom's.

How many inn signs of The Eagle and Child are there in the county? All of them are in areas where the Stanleys are, or have been, landowners.

The heraldic eagle once nested in Lathom Park; the babe was found not in its nest but at the foot of the tree. The story most likely to be the truth is this. The Lord of Lathom had no son born in wedlock but cunningly contrived to walk his lady through the Park one day to a grove of tall trees where a tiny infant of his begetting was waiting. On instruction, the baby's mother had dumped him there. The lady ran to pick him up. " Poor little mite ! Can I take him home to be companion for our own daughter? " she asked. Her husband agreed with alacrity.

Soon the boy, young Oskatel, had so far wheedled himself into his father's affections that he was about to alienate all the Lathom lands from the rightful heiress. She was betrothed to a Stanley. Always the Stanleys chose heiresses for their sons, so they very soon told the Lord of Lathom what he must do. Finally, he was diverted from his purpose and on his death Lathom came, in marriage, to the Stanleys, who adopted the eagle and child as a badge, as a constant reminder how easily it might have been lost to them.

Whilst there were Stanleys at Lathom there were Heskeths at a fair-built Hall by a Douglas ford. Rufford Hall today is safe in the bosom of the National Trust; from its tree-screened gardens where so soon the noise of passing traffic is cut out we are able to visit the Hall and enjoy the spacious rooms within, the banqueting hall with its roof supported by angel corbels with outspread wings, the quite magnificent movable screens or "spere" which, when the Heskeths entertained here, separated their guests from the confusion of kitchen and buttery.

The Hall is heavy with memories. Some think—and I wish it were proved true—that Shakespeare in the unaccounted-for years of his youth lived at Rufford, as a member of Sir Thomas Hesketh's Company of players. A William Shakeshaft, singing boy, was commended to Sir Thomas in the will of Alexander Hoghton of Lea near Preston in 1581. Was he with the Players at the wedding feast of Ursula Stanley at Knowsley in 1587, and was the poem "The Phoenix and the Turtle" composed there for her? Was the reason for his joining Fernando Stanley's strolling players the next year the result of a meeting at this wedding?

From Rufford the Douglas flows on, slowly, sluggishly, confined between floodbanks, to join the Yarrow and flow on to the estuary and the sea.

ROADS TO THE MOORS

These lead to the Yarrow and Douglas springs, four routes from the Bolton-Horwich-Chorley high road.

(1) From the Jolly Crofters, upper Horwich.

Turn along Georges Lane and take Matsmoor Lane on the right, rising to the heather moors. Paths ahead make for the valley of Dean Brook along the slope of Burnt Edge. Tracks galore wander on these heights, one to Two Lads and the ITA mast near which is the Douglas source and Scotsman's Stump, some waterlogged but taken by ramblers in their stride. Continue along Georges Lane as far as it goes. Rough drives penetrate the Bungalow grounds at the foot of the Pike; which climb, a short sharp pull to the Tower.

Or, make use of the new cement-grouted road to the ITA mast. Walkers have a good path from here, down to Belmont road and Wright's Arms by an Old Coal Road.

(2) From Horwich Crown or The Squirrel.

Through Lever Park the avenue heads for Rivington village, drives on the left hand drawing nearer to the Lake and the "ruins" of waterside castle, a copy of Liverpool's, long demolished, and those on the right hand making for Rivington Hall and Old Barn, with paths carrying higher into the Grounds and the Pike foot. From the village the road to Belmost passes, near the highest point, the Yarrow source.

(3) From the crossroads at Grimeford Lane.

A pleasant road, passing Headless Cross, wayside stocks and the group of old farms at Roscoe Lowe, a pleasing picture. The first road (right) is to Rivington village across the embankment. Walkers have a choice of two drives and tracks on each reservoir bank, both leading eventually to Knowley embankment and the upper Anglezarke reservoir. The young Yarrow is lost in the lake.

(4) From the Elephant and Castle, Babylon Lane.

The road to Heath Charnock forks to Rivington (right) and Anglezarke (left), and both open up country which, though man has wrought great changes on natural landscape, has much to commend it. The road with most variety crosses the Knowley embankment, follows the east shore of Anglezarke lake, climbs steeply from the quarries to the upper world. Attractive country stretches in all directions. The road reaches the lake again at its upper end, curves around the foot of Healey Nab and by taking a right turn down Hollins Lane comes to White Coppice. Tracks climb the moors. Roads leave for Chorley.

(5) A cross-country walk I took whilst writing this book, deciding one morning when I had missed the bus at Jolly Crofters near Horwich to walk home—at least as far as the outskirts of Blackburn. I started at 9; I was nearing Blackburn before 3 in the afternoon.

My route? Along Wallsuches, farm to farm from Harts Houses to Ormestones, in and out of Tigers Clough and up the pastures to the foot of the Tower above the Rivington Bungalow grounds. Lord Leverhulme built a road round Noon Hill into the Belmont-Rivington moor road; young curlews flying, sandpipers at pools in boggy ground, cotton grass a-flutter—and breezes to blow me along. Beyond Hordern Stoops a moorland path cuts off a corner into Belmont village. The traffic drove me to a farm track beyond the reservoirs, farm to farm under Old Man's Hill, and out on the Tockholes road above Holinshead Hall grounds. From the long road heading for the village I escaped to more footpaths, Higher Hill to Lower Hill, from the Manor house to Crow Trees, through the woodlands of Hole Bottom Clough to Whitehalgh farm, and arrived at Feniscowles by way of Stockclough lane. What variety for a short day's walk—and all in the "heart of industrial and darkest Lancashire"!

ROADS TO THE HILLS

These routes start from the Liverpool-Ormskirk-Preston highway. They cover country warm, cosy, friendly and altogether rural, with nothing of the hard-bitten quality of the moors about them.

(1) From Parbold—the lane passing Dalton church climbs to the

beacon surmounting Ashhurst Hill—and splendid prospects. Then carry on by the same high-level ridge road to Hall Green and see what history you can dig up around Upholland, in church and churchyard, at the Owl Inn and the courthouse with the Stanley arms on its walls.

(2) From Burscough Bridge and Parbold—climb the formidable brow passing the fine seventeenth-century hall of the Crispes, recently modernized, turning left along Robin Hood Lane, and left turn again to the grand viewpoint of High Moor. Then downhill by Harrock to Mawdesley. Look for the red willow growing acres, a return to the local production of raw material for the cane basket-weaving.

(3) From Rufford—go east through more willow fields to Black Moor lane at Mawdesley, pass the old Hall, Hell Hob (better known by this name than as Black Bull) and turn left along the road to Eccleston, where the fine old church stands by the Yarrow River. So to Croston or Chorley.

Rossendale Forest from Cliviger moors

III From Belmont Moors to Rossendale

HAVE YOU EVER been caught on the moors between Belmont and Turton or Holcombe when the sun is going down in a last spill of flame and fire? For a few minutes the landscape is transfigured and "beggars description". Then the sun dips, moorlands withdraw into dusk; the stars come out and down in the valleys "lamps multiply", whole constellations telling where the towns sprawl. Twilight brings with it a primitive melancholy in lonely places. What comfort the traveller has from "lighting-up time"!

So near to Darwen, Bury, Bolton, all this vast emptiness! A stranger to the north cannot credit it. He was not led to believe that Lancashire had any wide-open spaces.

Of course the general attitude about this region is "Not my cup of tea. Let's get on to Blackpool." I do not expect the countrylover for whom this is not home ground and therefore regarded with some affection to linger on these moors. As Dr. Johnson said it is "Worth seeing, but not worth going to see".

Only the Lancashire countrygoer can share Ammon Wrigley's love of it and feel "among these silent mystical moors—a sense of loneliness which is not loneliness, but the most exquisite companionship". You will find the heather, the bracken, the knolls, the hollows and the wide moorlands around you, "are holding some kind of converse of which not a syllable is heard but much felt".

We cannot expect non-northerners to share out enthusiasm for it, nor feel with the poet a hope that "they find the Saddleworth Hills in heaven". I know many "blue domers" in south-east Lancashire towns who "feel nearer God's heart" in the Pennine moors than anywhere else on earth.

Across south Lancashire from Rivington Pike and Anglezarke Moors to the Pennine watershed a series of long, flat-topped hills appear to be advancing, wave upon wave. All are between 1,250 and 1,500 feet, all stretch north to south, with short steep escarpment and long dip slope; between each ridge runs a river, a highway and a town, long drawn out. Above, the bare uninhabited heights and below, hollows crammed with narrow streets and factories—from which chimneys grow instead of trees. So sudden are the contrasts you can pass from one to the other extreme in a matter of minutes.

Stand in the town centres of Bacup, Haslingden or Rawtenstall and look up to the hills. In ten minutes you can be walking in a quiet world with no noise louder than a drumming snipe or a peewit screaming. There has always been a witchery here for those striding free with the bents, the short sweet grass or the turf under the soles of their stout shoes.

Once, though you can hardly believe it, the River Irwell, the most considerable stream in these parts, passing in and out of many a village and town on her way to Manchester, was a beauty queen. She had a good chance of winning the most beautiful river in Lancashire competition, organized by the river deities and reported by Michael Drayton, the Elizabethan marathon poet.

In Tudor times the "lovely Erwell" and her attendant nymphs, the pretty Tame, the Roch, the Spodden, Irk and Medlock, were as clear and bright as the Ribble.

> "In all your mirthful songs and merry meetings tell
> That Erwell every way doth Ribble far excell."

Look east from Rivington, Anglezarke or Darwen moors, but better still from Holcombe Hill, Musbury Tor or Thieveley Pike to overlook this moorland Lancashire.

Thieveley Pike is especially good. No hilltop gives wider prospects, which is why Celtic hillmen watched the dark depths of Cliviger and the wilds of Rossendale from the Dike they erected on its top for their defence. The Irwell begins its long journey from the southern side of the Pike; you can see her course unroll.

There is a good hill worth climbing from Egerton too, not far from the highway over Turton Moors, where the map marks "Druidical Circle", but all you will find is a sandy spot with a few scattered stones and a lonely wind-rippled pool among the heather tussocks. Prehistoric herdsmen met here for tribal lawmaking, for worship, for gathering and counting of their flocks. At times they must have cocked an eye at the view; tremendous! I heard someone say here, "I never thought England was that big!"

The best walking involves the tracking down of ancient highways. The Long Causeway, at least medieval monastic if not prehistoric, gives exciting views of Rossendale from across the Gorge of Cliviger. Limersgate, which takes the Haslingden Moors and the moortop near Darwen Tower in its stride, runs east-west as men defined it in the Bronze Age.

Driving the civilizing power of Rome through the north-west came Julius Agricola and his road builders in 79 A.D. Follow the line of the Manchester-Ribchester highway through Affetside and north by Blacksnape and Over Darwen.

The monks of Whalley, whose influence spread far and wide, travelled from the Abbey to their church of Saint Mariden, at Deane near Bolton, on the moorland track over Holcombe moors and a Pilgrims' Cross marked the way.

All these can involve the walkers in the best stuff of moorland tramping. There is nothing like it for bridging past and present.

Forest Days in Rossendale

A thousand years ago, when the Parish of Whalley and Blackburnshire were roughly synonymous, the boundaries took in Rossendale and its woodlands. Deansgreave, according to an old tale, was named where a Dean of Whalley in King Cnut's days slashed off a wolf's tail and so earned the nickname, Cutwolf.

Like the other Forests and Chases already mentioned, Rossendale passed in turn from Anglo-Saxon kings to William, the Norman de Lacys and, by marriage, to Thomas, Earl of Lancaster. Eventually the Duchy and Crown took over.

There were vaccaries here too, at Rawtenstall, Constablelegh, Crawshawbooth and Bacupbooth, all rented by William Leyland. Outside the actual forest bounds were communities of cowherds dwelling in the booths of Musbury, Yate and Pickup Bank. Leaseholders of king's land were well-known families, Pilkingtons of Rivington, Bartons of Smithills, Radcliffes of Radcliffe Tower; they held leases of New Hall Hey and Hoddlesden, among others, during the fifteenth century.

In the sixteenth century game had so decreased that foresters were redundant. Wolves, so much a menace in King John's days that 5s. was a reward for every head, had been completely cleared from haunts like Wolfenden and Wolfestones. Round Boarsgreave and Swinshaw there were no wild boars to be hunted. Very few deer now roamed on Deerplay Hill, Hartshead, at Stacksteads or Harthill.

Now tenants were encouraged to lease and farm the forest lands "for the greater increase of God's glory and the Commonwealth of this Realme", to carry on with the edifying and building of "houses and tents within the Forest—so that where beforetime there was nothing else but deer and other savage and wild beasts there is —grown to be a very good and fertile ground—very populous and well inhabited, and replenished with a great number of people".

What a journey Rossendale folk had every time they went to church at the castle chapel at Clitheroe! No wonder they pleaded in the most appealing terms they knew, for a church of their own. They built "new church in Rossendale" in 1511 when their piteous words had been heard by the king.

> "The way leading to the said parish church and the said forest is very foul painful and hillous and the country in the wintry season is so extremely and vehemently cold that the children and young infants in that time of year being borne to the church to be christened are in great peril of their lives, and almost starved with cold; the aged and impotent persons and women great with child, are not able to travel so far to hear the word of God—and the dead corpses there like to lie and remain unburied at such time as any that doth die and depart this world for lack of carriage."

The Holcombe Hunt

The Forest was no more, but did the local folk lose interest in blood sports? Not they, not in the Holcombe Hunt territory. It is no unusual thrill to see a quiet winter landscape spring to life as the harriers appear over a dark stone wall with the hunt galloping behind. A meet outside a village inn, anywhere between Hoghton and Brindle and the Pennines, and crowds appear as if by magic. The Point-to-Point, held at Harwood near Bolton, is a bigger draw every year. At Agricultural Shows the huntsman and hounds doing the round of the ring is a highlight.

Holcombe claims with pride that James I hunted with them during his three-day stay at Hoghton Tower in 1617, when the sporting gentlemen of the county went all out to show him good sport. A pack of deep-mouthed hounds was brought along from Quarlton

Manor by Sir Thomas Barton and so much did James enjoy his time with them that, in merry mood, he granted a Royal Warrant—the great privilege of wearing the King's own scarlet livery and the right to hunt so many days a week "for ever" in twelve townships being within the original forest bounds. But the hunt was in existence in Holcombe before this, and it still goes on.

From natives of Quarlton and Edgworth and any village around the moors it is possible to hear tales of the "old days" when masters knew their apprentices would be missing, and schoolmasters the scholars absent whenever the Hunt was up. Mourners carrying a bier in a funeral procession "downed it" and were away at the sound of the hunting horn, and "D'ye hear t'hounds!" cried the weaver at his loom, and away he went too.

> "When called the huntsman from the dale
> The mill folk ran away,
> For old and young in Saddleworth then
> Ne'er worked on a hunting day."

Saddleworth is some miles south, but the folk around Turton and Holcombe were made of the same stuff.

Legends of Old Rossendale

Every corner of the moorland region has not kept the traditions of the past nor has every spot the same power to evoke the past. Yet, where you think people are solely concerned with things of the present, like a bolt from the blue you find you are listening to one of those hair-curling tales which belong to a time when there was no radio or T.V.

I remember a W.I. meeting and a very old member, remembering.

Girls returning home along dark paths heard the patter of feet behind them—"Coming down from Thieveley I knew something were behind me—a big black dog, its eyes shining out of its head, and it never left me till I could see lights above Weir. My mam were looking out o't'door, waiting of me. Then I looked back and it had vanished!" A guardian spirit?

Rossendale is a hop, skip and jump over hill and valley from Pendle. It had its local witches too. I heard the strange tale of two farms on the slopes above the Irwell. At one were complaints of cream taken by thieving cats—not their own—night after night. In final desperation the farmer and his son decided to keep watch.

They saw the dairy door pushed open, a cat slink in and leap on to the stone shelf. Then they flung pans and pots at the intruder, which flew screeching out of the window. A few fields away a neighbouring farmer woke, as he often did, to find his wife missing. On this night his wife crept into the bedroom, her face bleeding, eyes blackened, arms scratched—— Everyone knew witches changed themselves into cats—or rats—or hares!

The devil was not unknown hereabouts. But worse than any devil were the "putters-out" from whom the handloom weavers received supplies of yarn. When the cloth was delivered to them they drove the hardest bargains, always keen to cheat the poor weavers of their due. One day a woman placed her "cut" on the putter-out's doorstep to be met with—"And didn't you hurry here as if th'Owd Lad were after thee?" To which she replied dryly, "Why be afeered of th'Owd Lad on t'Moors? I knew very well I'd find him here."

Rossendale is rich in local lore, collected a century ago by an historian of The Valley, Newbigging.

How did Hell Clough get its name? The Norse had this name for spouting falls, but Rossendale prefers to link it with the Devil. Th'Owd Lad lived near and enjoyed a morning dip in the lake at his door. When water was scanty he raised a good howling storm to augment his bath water. One day he went too far, his rainstorm sweeping down the Clough, tearing a breach in a gorge called The Thrutch, scattering rocks and boulders in its wake, enough to demolish a natural dam which impounded the waters of his favourite pool. In alarm he filled his apron ("brat" in the vernacular) with earth and stones to repair the breach, but his apron strings snapped and out fell his load. They say a mound near Stacksteads was the result. The devil never tidies up after himself!

"'There's a fine leet i'th'welkin,' as the witch o' Brandwood said when th'devil wur riding over Rossendale."

Antidote and charm against witchcraft: place a piece of oatcake under your pillow at night when you go to bed "and if it is eaten as soon as you wake, before opening your eyes, you will be safe from all black magic".

Sunday football in Crawshawbooth; some youths amusing themselves with a football in a field near Pinner Lodge and Sunnyside House were approached by a gentlemanly figure in black, who was apparently interested in the game. The ball came his way and, unable to resist it, he took it in his hand, kicked it and sent it spinning in the air. But it continued to rise until it vanished from the sight of the gaping lads. Turning to look at the stranger they espied—cloven hoof and barbed tail just visible under his cloak—and a moment later he had vanished in a blaze of fire!

Old Days—Good or Bad?

A hundred years ago, when Newbigging was writing his *History of Rossendale*, he was nearer to the wild days when witches were next-door neighbours and the devil was a familiar visitor. He knew the sons of the weavers who travelled the roads to the markets of Halifax or Colne or Manchester, in company for mutual protection against highway robbery and footpads.

Yet even today I have heard, in Lumb and Weir, of the precautions great-grandparents took when travelling to the markets with their bolts of cloth.

"I've heard tell how my great-grandfather would take a chopper from woodshed and lay it beside him in t'cart on t'driver's seat, saying, 'If any of them cloth thieves come up behind—this is what they'll get on their hands the moment they reach out—!'"

How often we hear tales of those who stole or attempted to steal cloth. Almost every family in the moorlands of Lancashire was concerned in the trade, the rich were clothiers, the ordinary folk spinners or weavers, or employed in the allied processes of fulling, bleaching, printing.

Looking north over the Gorge of Cliviger from the Rossendale heights called Carrs and Craggs the eye picks out scattered high-level farms near the ancient Long Causeway. At one, Hartley Royd, so I was told, was woven the cloth stolen by a local man who was executed for his crime at Halifax, the last victim of the dreaded " Maiden ".

Near the highway over Belmont Moors, at a cluster of old buildings called Horrocks Fold, was a bleach house—you can still see the low building, the culvert, clear spring water used in the bleaching process, and a croft behind where the cloth was " stented ". Theft of cloth from tenter grounds was so prevalent that it was among the most severely punished of crimes. The owner of this small concern was so determined to catch the thieves at work that he kept watch one night, swearing to shoot anyone he saw trespassing on the tenter field. It so happened that his son, returned from overseas, was coming home hoping to give his family a pleasant surprise. He travelled through the night and, taking a short cut across the familiar fields, was seen by his father. A shot was fired——

Local tragedies like this were long remembered.

So were the doings of poachers who got the better of the gamekeepers, and distillers of illicit whisky who were always one move ahead of the excise men.

The best stories of the making and disposing of " mountain dew ", outside Lakeland, come from the moors between Belmont and Darwen. The colliers, quarrymen and farmers were makers, consumers, distributors. Whole communities combined to thwart the excise men when the search was on.

This incident happened in the railway building days when navvies were working in the Sough tunnel north of Entwistle. One man had his "still" down in the tunnel itself—surely the safest of concealments. But the revenue officers got wind of it and, being particularly cunning, disguised themselves as labourers. They stepped into the crude lift and were lowered down one of the air shafts—but the manipulator guessed their identity. Instead of stopping the lift at the tunnel level and allowing them to step out, he went one farther—and deeper, sousing them in the sludge below. When he considered their ardour would be completely cooled they were hauled up again into the light of day. Their search was called off!

Turton is as good a village as any to collect such tales and bygones.

Moorland Villages—Turton and Edgworth

Turton is best approached from Bolton via Bradshaw, or from the highroad over the Moors, along a road called Greens Arms. Walkers tramp over the rough ground from Egerton, a choice of many old tracks, to Torra Barn and the railway bridge.

Torra names a farm with an outsize in barns; some say it stands on the site of the first settler. Or was it King Arthur, Ator, named Turton, as the over-romantic claim? The railway bridge is a Victorian whimsy, with battlements and turrets to be in keeping with the nearby Tower of Turton.

The Tower below the hill was first a stone peel of the Orrells, with walls of great thickness, a tower of refuge and defence to which, in Tudor times, an upper storey was added and black-and-white, half-timbered wings.

At Dove Hill, Turtonians of the past forgathered to enjoy cockings, dog fights, badger or bear baiting; there was a stone-built gazebo conveniently supplied with a cellar stocked with wine casks and beer barrels.

Behind is the slope of Chetham Close—a high pasture, part of the estate bought in 1628 by Humphrey Chetham (founder of the Library and Hospital, the Blue Coat School, in Manchester) and held by the same family until their descendants sold it in 1835 to James Kay.

A few years before the sale of the Tower and Manor the Turtonians decided it was high time the village which, for two centuries, had benefited from Humphrey Chetham's munificence should erect a

Turton Tower

fitting memorial to him. They hit upon the idea of a tower a hundred feet high within which would be spiral stairs, and were wondering whether a golden eagle or a statue of Master Humphrey would look best on top—when insufficient funds put an end to their dreams.

Would the moors have been improved by another landmark?

When the Turton U.D.C. are not meeting—what dignity their conferences must borrow from the setting—the caretaker shows interested visitors the old parts of the Tower. He will almost certainly tell of the early morning visit the Queen Mother paid, walking along the shady avenue from the Turton railway siding where the royal train was drawn up. "Queen Elizabeth slept here" is true—here!

Window in rear wall of Turton Tower

I am always glad Turton has not swept away all its old buildings. In the High Street the inn carries proudly the arms of Chetham, the old Grammar School is still there, a period-piece grocer's corner shop is a reminder of Victorian days, a tiny garden has the Turton Cross set back within it.

Some "oldster" relaxing on a garden seat is a repository of tales of the past when Turton Fair was the event of the year, when crowds thronged the main street and folk enjoyed every form of sport and pastime, including fighting and, formerly, a crude skirmishing in clogs called "up and down fighting". Stalls and booths lined the streets. Inns could not cope with the throng so every cottager turned provider and kept open house, inviting strangers indoors to sample the ham and eggs, hot-pot and potato pies.

One elderly woman I talked to one day, went through the verses of a song which sounded at Fair Days when gangs of lads ready for trouble chanted—

> "Now lads and have ye fowt?
> Nay we've not fowt yet.
> We'll have a walk round Chapeltown
> And muster up a set.
> We'll lay our clogs about 'em
> We'll make 'em gowp and stare,
> We'll tell 'em straight they'll have t' feyt
> If they come to Turton Fair."

East of Turton the deep valley is filled with reservoirs; across the water the hillside is cut by delphs, above which Edgworth's older houses appear against the skyline.

Here is another village with pockets of the past, not so much on the thoroughfare but in the many "Folds" a little off it. The villagers of three centuries ago lived in small groups of cottages near the large house of some yeoman farmer, or quarry owner, or chapman. The old road, parallel to the highway, links one with another. The Brandwoods named one tight little community, the Thomassons another and the John Horrocks, who bought land and opened a new delph in 1624, another. This last is perhaps most interesting.

Edgworth homestead, Horrocks Fold

Horrocks Fold is on an ancient paved way not far south of Hob Lane. In the eighteenth century John Horrocks was, like his forbears, a quarry owner and maker of millstones. His family of eighteen children numbered John and Samuel. John soon decided a fortune did not lie in following his father's footsteps. Instead he worked diligently at his weaving, sold his work in Preston, bought his own packhorses, became a trader—and eventually, opening the Yellow Mill in Preston, became one of the earliest manufacturers and founder of the firm whose cotton products are world famous.

In writing his *Path to Rome*, Hilaire Belloc wrote of the vast system of Roman roads which from our northern moortops he saw unrolling themselves in all their order till he could see "Europe and Rome shining at the end".

The road from Ribchester to Manchester was "the road home" to old soldiers. I wonder what they felt about it?

The Roman way passing from Edgworth over the hills, quite direct to Wayoh and Over Darwen I have already mentioned (page 173). It is a good road for seeing Lancashire as others imagine it, but transfigured by a blaze of evening lights in winter.

Such a feast of lights; it should make illuminations at Blackpool and Morecambe unnecessary!

A South African friend was "misguided" on leaving Manchester, being directed to the Ribble valley by roads through the heart of Rossendale, Bury, Ramsbottom, Haslingden. Night fell and he was still far from Whalley. The valleys thick with towns glittering with lights impressed him profoundly, but more so the moors, empty as the veldt.

Moorland Routes

Use O.S. one-inch map, Sheet 95.

(1) From Turton Moors highroad.

From the Globe Inn, Egerton, enquire for the track to Butterworth farm and so up to the Druidical Circle for the views if not for archaeology. Or follow the uphill track to Torra Barn and Turton.

(2) From Green Arms Lane, 2 miles south of Darwen, explore the almost lakeland landscape below, by a path near the water. Or a mile along the road strike the track over high pastures which ends at Turton station. Or turn from the lane to discover the pockets of history at Entwistle, several ancient homesteads, and Crow Trees on a lakeland peninsula doomed to be drowned.

(3) East of the Roman Road and Edgworth; hills and moors to infinity. One of the ancient footways above Holcombe Brook follows the lower slope of Harcles Hill, the track climbing higher on the moor at Bull Hill, this the Whalley monks' and abbey pilgrims' route which finally drops into the valley at Helmshore or Haslingden.

(4) East of Edenfield and north of Rochdale; take to your feet over stark moors where many once well-used routes crisscross the rough ground of Hailstorm Hill. Or stride out for Rooley Moor "with the sunlight in your faces", climbing by the little Spodden River to Top of Pike and the moor top inn. Generations knew the former inn on the lonely heights, a rendezvous for many, not only in summer but at midwinter. New Year's Day was when tough types forgathered for Rooley Moor races.

No need to avoid the moor on New Year's Days in this decade.

The old scenes are not re-enacted. I doubt if many even recall the old ballad—

> " As I were going on Rooley Moor,
> And Rooley Moor it shaked,
> I saw twelve men running—
> And all stark naket ! "

Which was rather more than breaking the ice on the Serpentine !

(5) I leave to the last the hill road which was the most familiar to all travellers of the distant past, an important link between Lancashire and Yorkshire, Manchester and Halifax. For many journeying from the east of the Pennines it was their first sight of Lancashire and because, even in Tudor times, strangers approached our borders with misgivings, ready to endure and with little hope of enjoyment, many quailed as they poised on the watershed.

Blackstone Edge, The Edge, the formidable crossing of the English Alps ! Leave Rochdale for Littleborough and, taking the Old Blackstone Edge Road, a right fork by a wayside hostelry passing the rock-sited Windy Bank, hall of seventeenth-century Lightowlers, return to the main highway and climb direct to the skyline. Or, better still, walk the paved causeway to the right of it sited on the Roman Way, part of the road of the legionaries and from the windbattered rock ramparts of the summit, or the relative calm of Robin Hood's Bed " where winds never blow", decide for yourself whether Lancashire deserves the judgment of those who use " dreary, drab, bedraggled " to describe her landscape.

Setting out on his journey out of Yorkshire, William Camden began by saying:

> " I must now turn the course of my journey another way, unto the rest of the Brigantes, who were planted on the farther side of the Hilles toward the Irish Sea; and first into Lancashire which I go unto (God speed me well) after a sort somewhat against my will——"

That was Lancashire unseen. He travelled across the county finding more and more nice things to say.

And so be it with all countrygoers, not Lancastrian, who follow my book.

" Hey for Lancashire ! "

INDEX

Index